THE ELEMENTS OF EFFORT

THE
ELEMENTS
OF
EFFORT

Reflections on the Art and Science
of Running

John Jerome

BREAKAWAY BOOKS
NEW YORK CITY
1997

The Elements of Effort:
Reflections on the Art and Science of Running

ISBN: 1-55821-614-6
Library of Congress Catalog Number: 97-74482

Published by Breakaway Books
P. O. Box 1109
Ansonia Station
New York, NY 10023
(212) 595-2216
(800) 548-4348

Breakaway Books are distributed to the trade by:
The Lyons Press
31 West 21st Street
New York, NY 10010

FIRST EDITION

CONTENTS

SPRING

SUMMER

FALL

INTRODUCTION

The heart is the tachometer of effort.

A lot of writers I know keep a small book called *The Elements of Style* on a shelf right over their desks. Only seventy-one pages long, it is a perfect gem of advice on clear composition, and an entertaining read in the bargain. It's handy to have around.

It was written by William Strunk Jr., a professor of English at Cornell, in 1918, intending "merely to give in brief space the principal requirements of plain English." One of Strunk's students was E. B. White, who went on to become one of the most graceful essayists in American letters. In 1959, White revised what Will Strunk always called his "little book," added an introduction, and had it republished. It has never since gone out of print. Writers refer to simply it as "Strunk and White."

As a runner and a writer I've always thought we needed a similar basic guide to the principles of athletic training. Ideally it would be expressed not in the Tab-A-in-Slot-B manner of most exercise physiology texts, but with a little more sympathy for the reader—a sentiment acquired from Strunk and White. "Will felt that the reader was in serious trouble most of the time," said White, "a man floundering in a swamp, and that it was the duty of anyone attempting to write English to drain the swamp quickly and get his man up on dry ground, or at least throw him a rope."

For fourteen years I've written *The Complete Runner's Day-by-Day Log and Calendar*. In composing the monthly essays for the *Log,* I've tried to gather the most useful principles of athletic effort, weave them into a comfortable form, and link them to the larger phenomenal world in which we run. The principles do not represent all one might ever possibly want to know about athletic training, but if your eyes tend to glaze over at discussions of VO_2 max—or yet another formula for computing the heart-rate range at which the training effect allegedly kicks in— what follows is an attempt to toss you a few of Will Strunk's handy ropes.

Runners are able to run because the body turns food into a molecule that comes with a kind of magnet attached to it. The magnet, a free phosphate radical, leaps to make new attachments, and in that leap releases energy, which powers muscle, which drives us down the road. This may not be the most interesting transaction in the world—except perhaps for chemistry majors—but its elemental nature is worth keeping in mind.

Running is the most elemental sport there is. We are genetically programmed to do it. One might even say we are the free-ranging, curious, restless creatures that we are because of running. Surely our instinct for freedom is a legacy of this essential mobility.

I think freedom itself is the source of running's great appeal. Slip on a pair of shoes, slip out the door, and you're there: free. No commute to a playing field, no teams or uniforms, no dates to arrange. No score-keeping, no rules, no fancy equipment to buy. Try though the gimmick-sellers have to complicate the sport, nothing has compromised running's essential simplicity.

Simplicity, however, is a quality that, in human affairs, is difficult to hang on to. As instinctively as we are driven to run free, we are also driven to analyze and assess, to pry apart, to deeply know. Just as we have marketeers dreaming up new running fads and fashions, we have scientists—and a thousand treadmills—searching out the innermost secrets of human performance, and coaches shepherding their guinea-pig athletes through practical trials of those secrets. We can't possibly know too much about a given subject—to claim that is to deny our curiosity, which is an essential part of our humanness—but sometimes it feels as if we do. *The Elements of Effort* is intended as a celebration of running's original simplicity. It is an attempt to illustrate, in familiar essays, the elemental aspects of running.

You do every day's run on your feet, but you also do it in your head. The pieces that follow acknowledge that fact; they are therefore unapologetically personal, as personal as I can make them. Each is a line of thought that came to me while running, that gave me a chance to let my mind go off and play. I hope you'll find in them a suitable collection of ideas to mull over in the course of your own daily runs.

The *Log* from which many of the ideas in this book spring was originated by Jim Fixx in 1979, two years after he published his masterpiece, *The Complete Book of Running*. That was easily the most popular running book of all time, and after more than twenty years is still the one responsible for getting most of us started in the first place. *The Elements of Effort* is dedicated to Jim's memory.

—John Jerome

I

WINTER

GIFTS

The greatest gift that running has given me —after continuing health, a daily visit to my interior life, and a warm feeling for everyone else who enjoys the sport—is what might be called a sympathy for physiology. Not in the poor-baby sense of sympathy, but in the isn't-that-wonderful sense. The training effect itself —the body's natural improvement in response to stress—is the most delicious small piece of physiology I know. I wouldn't have learned about it if it weren't for running.

BLAH

"Whenever I find myself growing grim about the mouth," says Ishmael, in the well-known opening scene of *Moby-Dick,* "whenever it is a damp, drizzly November of the soul . . . I account it high time to get to sea as soon as I can." Couldn't Ishmael have just gone for a run instead?

That would be running as mechanism for deliberate psychological change—or, as we used to say, blowing the cobwebs out. Stride off down the road, get the joints loose and the kinks out. Break a little sweat: heck, it'll even help lubricate that winter-dried skin.

Too bad the weather is so determined not to cooperate. Faced with deep winter, the unfortunate question becomes, how bad do the jimjams have to get to drive us out there where we can do the actual running? Where I live, the only thing more dependably rotten than the winter blahs is the weather itself. There's all this water coming down, in one miserable form or another. About the only way I can get myself going is to summon up a steely determination to go enjoy the earth. Somehow that frame of mind makes it easier to get out the door.

Fortunately for that practice the seasons themselves are among the most entertaining things about the earth—if you can just back off far enough to get the right perspective on them. Think of it: seasons are the product of nothing more than the planet's tilt and wander, its slightly whopperjawed displacement from even keel. It is only because the hemisphere we run in happens, at this time of the year, to lean back away from the sun—weakening its effect through these more or less miserable months— that the nights get so long and the days so cold, the weather systems so powerful (and the forecasts so much less reliable).

That our planet is deposited in space just slightly off kilter is therefore precisely what keeps things in constant change. And that's what keeps the earth refreshing itself, so it doesn't stabilize, grow stagnant, and die. The wobble in the planet's flight makes the seasons, which bring the water (in our faces or not), which in turn keeps the earth not only full of life but also beautiful. I love that: the earth is beautiful because of water. And the movement of that water from place to place is exactly what keeps the whole operation viable.

This may not be the ultimate consolation when one of those ten-degree, ten-mph winds is driving water, in the form of icicles, down your neck. All you want is a nice relaxing run, and the atmospherics insist on turning it into the next thing to a polar expedition. Deep winter may not always present the most salutary conditions for runners, but think of it this way: change is what keeps us fresh too. Go for a run, change your life. Sometimes it can work better in February than it does in June.

RUNNING VS. TRAINING

There is running to run and there is running to train, and the difference between the two approaches can best be summed up by a single word: increase. Training is about trying to get more. So is all the rest of sport, all competition. In the running sports, what we're trying to get more of is speed (or more distance covered for a given time, same thing), but for any sport the goal is some equivalent gain. You might say that those of us who run to train see life as a kind of graph, and concern ourselves primarily with the angle of its line.

Running just to run, on the other hand, is about sustaining. Those of us who are not trying to improve are running for the experience itself, and the only pressure we place on ourselves is to be able to continue. We see life as a block of time, and concern ourselves with how best to fill it. The motivation is entirely different.

No judgment, moral or otherwise, is intended in this division. Most of us, I think, have some experience with both approaches, and may switch groups at will. There are plenty of purely recreational runners who go at their sport with an intensity and seriousness that puts would-be

Olympians to shame, just as there are racers who find in competition a lighthearted escape from seriousness—and who achieve no less success for their carefree approach.

Recreation sometimes gets a bum rap. The word tends to conjure up spas and toys and sports equipment, but recreation is, or should be, about having a good time. Make that *having good time:* spending our minutes and hours at a high level of quality experience. Running—or any other effortful gross-motor activity, extended over time—is a powerful tool for keeping ourselves in the present tense, and the present tense is always a vacation. Vacations are restorative—unless, perhaps, we go at them competitively.

But to say that is to give competition a bum rap too. Too often we equate competitiveness with overweening ambition, with ruthlessness, even with greed. It can be a vehicle for these traits, but it can also be a crucible for refinement of that grand old Victorian notion, now almost absent from our vocabularies, of character. If nothing else, competition will teach us, inevitably, how to lose. To learn what losing really means—and does not mean—may be as important a lesson as we are privileged to get.

Running just to run, however, does take a little different mind-set: you have to start seeing your life as a block of time, rather than a line on a graph.

POINTLESSNESS

A lot of runners use the daily energy burn as an excuse for eating everything in sight. Why worry about a bedtime bowl of ice cream when you're deliberately going out and spending a thousand extra calories a day? This is the sin of volume.

There are also runners who shrink in horror from particular poisons (white bread, white sugar, white martinis) and gobble particular magic potions (vitamin C, bee pollen, raw things) in search of an edge. This is the sin of pointlessness. You don't power your muscles with wheat germ or bee dung, you power your muscles by breaking glycogen into adenosine triphosphate and pyruvic acid. It takes place at the level of carbon and hydrogen and phosphorus, not at the level of kelp or tofu or even french fries.

All these years they've been telling you that you are what you eat. That's wrong. You aren't what you eat, you are what you do.

PATIENCE

Physical change takes place at the level of the cell. That's why nothing in training is more important than patience.

THE WEB

The body comes in one flexible piece. If you don't understand it that way, and treat it that way, you're asking for trouble.

The material that ties the body into one piece is connective tissue—tendon and ligament, yes, but also muscle sheath, organ lining, bone covering, bone itself, and all the rest of the structural material of the body. It is the ground structure, the body's organizing principle.

Apply force to it at any point and it transmits the resulting stresses throughout the body. At the most straightforward level—as in tendons— it carries the force generated in the muscle across the hinge of the joint to move the bone on the other side. But the transmission of force is seldom that simple. Most joints are supplied with multiple muscle-tendon units that work together. During heavy efforts and complex motions, the load is distributed among several muscle groups. Injury to one muscle will force the others to compensate, overloading them. Muscles pull in straight lines; when they must substitute for an injured partner, they work their connective tissues at new angles, out of the usual alignments, dragging tendons across joint crossings and loading attachment points in unaccustomed directions. Thus the tension—the load—spreads out beyond the injured unit. Tendon injuries have a way of begetting tendon injuries, and so on, throughout the one-piece body.

Even a few days with, say, a sore ankle will be recorded elsewhere. When you limp you favor one calf muscle, loading the other. The underloaded calf begins to weaken. (Atrophy from disuse starts within six hours of immobilization of a joint.) The overloaded calf grows stronger. Compensating for the strength differential at the calf, you load thighs and hips differently; one side gradually grows stronger with work, the other weaker with inactivity. The effect spreads and widens to the muscles of the spine. When the muscles on one side of the spine are strong and the other side weak, you are forced to change the way you generate and apply force in every direction.

Thus the injury is imprinted throughout the body, traces of it remaining after the injury itself is healed. The medium in which the traces are laid down and through which the message is transmitted is connective tissue. The traces can take the form of everything from scar tissue to malformed bone, from reduced range of motion to impaired cardiac function.

Injuries only emphasize the mechanism; the forces are being transmitted whether you are injured or not. To continue running over the long haul, you have to accommodate them. The job is management of the body; you'll do better if you manage it as one flexible piece.

THE OTHER HALF

We train the muscles by contracting them; stretching is the uncompleted half of every muscle contraction. It is critical to the muscle's health.

So don't stretch to the point of pain, don't stretch to stretch the unstretchable, don't stretch to increase your range of motion. Just stretch to stretch your muscles. Stretch because it feels good. You'll run longer and more comfortably that way, and probably faster, too.

EFFICIENCY

There may be insignificant small manner-
isms that differentiate one good runner's
stride from the next, but essentially, all good
runners run the same way. The body is quiet,
the head still, the arms pump only enough
to provide adequate counterbalance. There's
no excessive or violent motion anywhere, no
bobbing up and down, the feet lifted no higher
than required to get the job done. Everything
is smooth.

Work for smoothness if you will, but don't
worry too much about style. The ineluctable
laws of physics—and the pain of fatigue—will
always, eventually, trim away the waste motion
and stylistic quirks.

COLD

You may live in the sunny Southland or on
the Left Coast, or somewhere else where wintry
blasts are only a rumor, but most of us runners
have at least a small climatological problem:

cold. I live in New England, and I speak from frigid experience. Running in extreme cold is exhilarating most of the time, if the footing isn't too icy, but it does require a judicious approach, a little different attitude.

Cold affects athletic performance in ways we may not always think about. A few years ago I watched—on TV, thank God—a pro football game played in zero weather, with brutal winds. Football certainly isn't running, but the ex-jocks who did the broadcast kept reminiscing about playing the game in severe cold. I found their observations—memories, really—to be fascinating.

They pointed out, for example, that despite the hard work, the players do lose heat from their body core—that is, hypothermia begins to set in. You burn off energy just staying warm, which leaves less energy for the job at hand. You get tired more quickly. Hypothermia brings on shivering, which makes it hard to focus on specific tasks—and hard to summon up fine-motor control. Your hands lose suppleness and feeling, so manual skills—throwing the ball or catching it, or even just holding on to it—get harder and harder. The ball itself gets slick, doesn't have any give to it, feels like a rock. The prospect of having to kick it is positively frightening, particularly if your feet are already aching from the cold.

In fact everything you do hurts. Because of that, your movements become restricted. You lose range of motion. You get tentative. While your own physical scale of action is reduced, however, the field actually begins to play a little larger than usual. This in turn changes the physics of the game—all those angles and distances and dimensions that you practiced with. The athletes have to adjust to this. All of the athletes in a cold-weather performance have to adjust to the same changes, of course, but the ones who can adjust best, or most quickly, will have an advantage.

Not that runners have to deal with problems in kicking, catching, or throwing; a lot of these concerns wouldn't seem to apply to our sport. But physics are physics, and the larger problem of the athletic body at work in a frigid environment is in many ways the same. These are the class of problems, you might say, that the runner has to solve. Thinking about them in this way may not help you get started on a miserable morning, but it can guide you to safer, more enjoyable runs once you manage to talk yourself out the door.

FIRST PRINCIPLES

You run up the hill for your heart, down the hill for your legs.

CHILD'S PLAY

Somehow my running keeps getting serious on me. I feel like I've lost the right to decide just to enjoy it. I get hung up on distances, or not missing a day, or the health benefits. (Whatever happened to the happiness benefits?)

I have to remind myself not just to stick to my side of the road and grind it out, but to go leap ditches and climb hillocks, to bushwhack, to break out of that rigid plodding that is good for the coronary arteries but not necessarily for the heart or the soul. To go ahead, every once in a while, and jump in that puddle with both feet. It takes conscious thought to keep play in our running.

HAPPINESS

After all these years, and all these millions of runners, the nonrunning press still shows occasional hostility toward the sport. No part of the press does so more consistently than sportswriters themselves. And nothing that uncomprehending sportswriters can find to say is any sappier than the complaint that we don't look happy when we run.

This noncomprehension is surely willful. Sportswriters seek simplicity, explanations, unquestioned outcomes. A hanging curve that gets knocked over the fence, the long bomb over the safety's head, are powerful explanations of why one team and not the other won the contest. Even who crosses the finish line first—never mind why—is acceptably unambiguous, although track sports, eschewing violence along with sticks and balls, are perilously close to a nonsport in most sportswriters' eyes. But running itself—for recreation, for pleasure, never mind about health or even athletic training—is incomprehensible to the sportswriting mind. If nobody wins, how do you tell when you're done?

You can't really blame the writers for focusing on results: they have to have something to print. You also can't blame the athletes, in any sport, for their natural distrust of the press. Athletes know that sports start with play, with process; writers for some reason have trouble comprehending that. Athletes know that it's the doing, not the winning, that keeps you coming back. This has even been institutionalized, in the old cliché about it mattering not whether you win or lose but how you play the game. Unfortunately it was a writer, not an athlete, who did the institutionalizing, and he missed the point. *How* you play the game implies a moralistic judgment; the athlete knows it's simply *that* you play the game: getting out and experiencing it. The quality of play, like winning, is a side issue. The pleasure of the effort is what keeps sports alive.

Another cliché says that most writers don't want to write, they want to have written: the doing is too painful. Maybe that's why they misunderstand running. Stuck for another column, they growl about the pained expressions they see on the faces of the runners. It's sportswriting's version of "If you're so smart, why aren't you rich?" If running is so much fun, then why are runners always grimacing so? How can it make you happy when I can tell just by looking that it hurts?

These astute observers have never noticed that violinists, for example, also usually look unhappy, at the very moments when they are re-creating some of the most soaring triumphs of human creativity. Winning quarterbacks look unhappy, for goodness' sake, right up to the final gun. A happy smile is a result, like a final score.

We smile in the shower; while we're running, we're too busy having fun. Too busy being happy to smile about it.

GOING LONG, GETTING LONGER

Aging is a deterioration of connective tissue. The stiffness, shrinkage, and drying up of aging occur directly in that great web of fiber that ties us together. What exercise does is resist this stiffening. Most of those complex physiological processes that we call training come down, at bottom, to maintaining the lively resilience of our connective tissue. Age is what makes it tight, movement is what keeps it loose. If you can't stay young, stay loose.

Muscle has a bad reputation. We speak of it as the opposite of brains, a synonym for brute force and insensitivity. But no thought can be acted upon nor any pleasure enjoyed without muscle's help: we can't breathe, eat, drink, make love, or maintain life without it. We give credit to nerves for sensory richness, but without muscle to process stimuli, those nerves would have little to work on. (Sensors adapt quickly to a constant stimulus. We use movement to keep the stimuli varied. The movement comes from muscle.) Besides, living muscle is among the loveliest substances on earth to look at, to touch, and above all to put to use.

Furthermore, it's not dumb, not at all: muscle has great intelligence, a product of its dual function. We think of muscle as the stuff with which we do things, but it is also the stuff that tells us what is done to us and what we do to ourselves. Nerves run from the muscle as well as to it; it is as much a sensor as it is an effector. The musculature is a suit of power draped over our otherwise helpless bones, but it is also a suit of sensitivity, assessing our situation, helping us react to the world's requirements.

Muscle's capacity for delivering information was driven home to me vividly on a late-night flight in a rear seat on a commercial aircraft. Looking up the long aisle, I watched the airplane's nose lift and drop, swing from left to right and back again. Then I realized I was seeing nothing of the sort: with total darkness outside, I could see nothing change its position in relation to anything else. There wasn't any movement to see. I was notified of the plane's changes in attitude in small part by the balance mechanism in my inner ear and the skin of my backside, but mostly by my musculature, feeling gravity and momentum tug at my body mass from new angles. My brain translated what I felt into visual change. I'd have sworn I was seeing it happen.

The senses, like the body, are all one piece. Close your eyes and hold your nose, they say, and your mouth can't tell apple from raw potato. The traditional five senses are inventions—ideas, really—out of science's continuing struggle to understand by reduction. It is true that we are capable of singling out one kind of information at a time from the swirl of experience that the world is throwing at us, but that doesn't mean we're not still receiving the rest of that information, or that information from other sensors isn't augmenting and coloring the information to which we're paying attention. The senses reside in the brain's interpretation, not in the nerve endings.

We do relish the swirl of information. Our evolution as a culture has largely been devoted to finding more and more sophisticated ways of firing off those sensory neurons. All our arts and leisures are products of that search. Firing off the sensory neurons of our musculature—making fuller use of that huge sensory organ that is human muscle—is a terrific pleasure. We call it play, or, in its more organized form, athletics.

LISTENING TO THE MAN

A Canadian study asked subjects if their reasons for exercising were social, health-related, cathartic (stress-relieving), or aesthetic (as in a better-looking body). The men ranked catharsis first, the women aesthetics. There's a somewhat cynical view—untested, so far as I know—that the entire fitness boom is really fueled by the pursuit of better sex. Perhaps the Canadian men are using exercise in place of sex—and the women in search of a little more.

Another Canadian survey compared ten motivating factors for being physically active. "The fitness leader's advice" came in dead last.

GETTING OFF YOUR OWN BACK

Finding the pleasure in hard physical work is easy (that's what the fitness "craze" has always been about); keeping it pleasurable is the hard part. This is the soberest message to come out of modern studies of fitness. The unfortunate truth is that nearly everyone who starts getting positive results from exercise eventually over-does it. If you push too hard, the wear and tear gets too damned specific. Recovery time is critical. Overuse injuries are our pesky new plague.

Work hard, the exercise physiologists are now saying, but don't work too much. After decades of telling us to get off our duffs, now they're saying okay, great, but don't go crazy. Get out there and tire yourself, but don't come to love it too much, this tiring out. Understand the physiology, the better to avoid injury. Know where the pleasure—and the pain—come from.

WARMING UP, COOLING DOWN

The advice that comes showering down on us in the popular literature—from coaches, trainers, and other interpreters of exercise physiology—may not quite go in one ear and out the other, but the only way to make it really stick is to put it to some kind of test. When we do, we turn it into a set of sensations that we not only feel while they're going on but can remember afterward. Until we do, advice is just words.

Warming up and cooling down fit into this category for me. I've been told about careful warm-ups all my life, but I've had trouble making myself take the time. Or I did until I trained hard enough and regularly enough to get hit in the face with the difference between physiological warmth and cold. Until I knew the difference not with my head but with my aching muscles.

"Muscles," in that sense, is athletic slang for a complicated physiological kit. Yes, warm muscle works better and gets injured less, just like they're always telling us. But it isn't just muscle, it is tendon and ligament and the rest of the connective tissue, it is joint lubricants and all the other fluids. That sluggishness you feel is not in your head, it's in the very viscosity of your blood. The warm-up applies profitably even to nerve tissue, synapses, supplies of neuro-transmitters. It is simply the best means we have of sweeping out the residues of both use and disuse, the unresolved products of yesterday's hard work or sloth.

The same goes for cooling down, of course. Skipping that step can be dangerous. Exercise generates adrenaline, which helps bring the heart rate up; an abrupt halt to exercise doesn't give the system time enough to shut down the adrenaline, which can drive the heart into dangerous arrhythmias. And if difficult accommodations at the hormonal level don't catch your attention, then perhaps you might want to envision the condition in which you're leaving the larger systems when you shut them down too quickly: all those soft tissues engorged with wastes, spasmodic with fatigue.

The real action, however, is down there among the bits of chemistry. What training finally teaches us is to comprehend things like the warm-up and the cool-down at the cellular level, even the molecular level. The processes that we are most interested in work better, and improve faster, if brought carefully up to speed and carefully back down to normal use.

BELIEF SYSTEMS

Cold itself is no real problem, since running generates body heat. Wind is different. Weathercasters are fond of astonishing us with frightful, and not always believable, wind-chill factors. Runners should believe.

DANCING WITH FATIGUE

All running, all exercise—all work, for that matter—is a dance with fatigue: manipulation of it, experimentation with it, and, finally, acceptance of it. What training is for is to pull its teeth.

A manageable level of fatigue is a useful training tool. It encourages you to relax, lets you seek out the gentlest and most efficient stride. Until you're in shape the first unpleasant signals of fatigue insist that things are going to deteriorate quickly and you're going to grind to a halt; after you're in shape those same signals only remind you to reestablish homeostasis. Stabilize at this higher level of output, and then, with your fatigue well in hand, you discover you can go on—and on and on.

Even purely recreational runners can thus come to know what racers know: that the most enjoyable times in running come when you are teetering on the edge of fatigue but hang on a moment longer, and a moment longer, and at some point discover not only that you can bear it but that you can even pick it up a bit.

That is the greatest thrill in endurance athletics —a greater thrill, even, than winning. And it is available to the totally noncompetitive recreational runner, so long as you're willing to avail yourself of the opportunity—the freedom—to experiment with levels of fatigue.

ROAD THOUGHTS

A physiological point of view is only one more tool for getting a firmer grasp on the running experience, but it's a good one. Physiology can be a kind of mental pry-bar for thinking about your running experience. For thinking about all your experience, for that matter: get in the habit and you'll find, for example, that it illuminates the efforts of other athletes, enriching your enjoyment of all sports, participatory or otherwise.

It can also change the way you understand your nonathletic efforts, the other work you do. Energy supply, fluid balance, muscle tension, biomechanical efficiency, management of the products of fatigue—these are problems of the everyday workplace too, although we seldom think of them that way. We can come to understand their processes more clearly from dealing with them on the road. From thinking about them as we deal with them on the road.

SHIVERING

If you shiver when you slow down, seek shelter and warmth. Shivering is a sign your extremities are using up heat that your vital organs need to keep you alive.

THE PHYSIOLOGY OF CONFIDENCE

One of the puzzling findings of fitness research is that running improves overall confidence. I don't doubt it happens, but I've never quite figured out how. Why should knowing that you can run X distance at Y pace translate into other aspects of your life? Is it simply that feeling better gives you a more bullish outlook?

Athletes tend to look at the subject from the other direction: confidence improves running, improves performance in any sport. Coaches will tell you it is as important to athletic success as skill. You'll never perform at your best if there's anything tentative in your approach to your task. Unsureness saps strength; hesitancy throws off timing; self-doubt erodes will. Just as you can feel the confidence in a good violinist's notes—hitting them dead on, knowing full well what to do with them—you can perceive it in the movements of a good athlete. A pole-vault coach once told me he can tell from the sound of the approach run whether it's going to be a good vault or not. No need to watch: a confident vaulter's last three footfalls say, right out loud, that he's hit his marks and is accelerating through the box.

This sounds like that pop-psych motivational stuff that coaches love so much, but there may be physiology involved. You can train confidence into your muscles—or into your tendons, anyway. There's an organ for it, called the Golgi tendon organ. It's a much more sophisticated nerve ending than we used to think.

The Golgi tendon organ is traditionally described as a protective device, signaling excessive load. When a muscle begins to pull too hard on its tendon, Golgi organs make it let go to prevent injury: a reflex fires and the muscle abruptly relaxes, in what's called a "clasp-knife response." The sudden victory in arm wrestling comes when the loser's Golgi organs kick in. (It isn't infallible; fractures are not unheard of.)

When you're learning a new athletic motion, it is follow-through that gives trouble. New movements mean unfamiliar muscle loadings, which fire the protective response, stopping contraction, killing the motion prematurely. It's a peculiarly helpless feeling. You have to learn the new move before you can put much force into it. You have to "groove" it, which means, in part, training the Golgi organs to accept higher loadings.

You train the Golgi organs by working them, of course—contracting muscles, using your strength, familiarizing yourself with higher tendon loadings. When you do, you not only raise the force they can exert before that helpless feeling kicks in, but you also begin to know more accurately where your limbs are going when you move them. You are better able to predict what is likely to happen when you make an effort. You become grounded, more stable, better able to react to the requirements of the physical world.

In fact that helpless feeling—that queasy sense of being lost in the middle of a motion, all strength and control suddenly gone—is a perfect physical metaphor for psychological loss of confidence. Getting rid of it must be how running, or any other athletic training, builds confidence. The more you move yourself by your own muscle power, no matter what form that movement takes, the surer you will be of the result. That's a definition of confidence.

RAIN IN THE FACE

Snow is falling with what my wife describes as grim efficiency, and I am delaying my run, hoping for a break. Running in a snowstorm can be fun, if you don't mind lousy traction underfoot and a general soaking, but I'm finding it hard to get over the threshold, so to speak. I'll probably enjoy it once I get going.

I would like to state unequivocally, however,

that I don't like rain in the face, even when it's rearranged into beautiful snowflakes. Rain in your face, as pleasure, is a romantic notion out of childhood, I think. For reasons of age if not of disposition, I am postromantic in physical matters. I used to be one of those nuts who likes to dive into cold water first thing in the morning—until I moved to a place that had a pond. Now it's always available (when not frozen) and lies there accusing me every summer morning of my life.

This does not mean that I am past enjoying the experience of weather. I am still fascinated by the physics of snow, of snowstorms, rainstorms, even dust storms. Storms always make me think what a wonderful planet this is, to have developed this method of continual redistribution of its surface materials: disturbances powered by the sun, by nothing more than heat and light. The weather is a daily demonstration of how variety is kept in the world, how the physical realm regularly reorganizes itself in the name of that diversity that strengthens it and provides its vitality.

The other thing I like about snow or rain, about weather in general, is that it is exactly as it presents itself to us. It is not tweaked, not given some spin to fit someone else's ulterior motive. There is no advertising; these are the conditions that obtain. Experiencing this clearly and directly, unmodified by the distractions of the modern world, is worth something. I find it helps to think about these things when the stuff is hitting you in the face.

TWENTY-ONE DAYS FROM NOW

At any given time you're in shape for what you were doing two weeks ago. There is roughly a twenty-one-day cycle to the training process, and we're always at day eleven. If you begin by jogging around the block every day, in eleven days you'll have accommodated to that work-load (it gets easier), and after twenty-one days you'll have got all the training effect you're going to get out of a one-block jog.

If you're driven by the self-improvement bug, you then have to increase the work load—run faster or farther, or carry more weight. If jogging comfortably around the block is sufficient for your ambitions, you can cruise—maintain, in other words—thereafter, and probably enjoy it.

The first eleven days of any new cycle may

well be uncomfortable, however. The various body parts and systems do resent it when their load is increased, and they let you know. Their resentment will fade, but only if you push past it.

RESCUE

If you're having trouble staying motivated, seek an attitude adjustment. Stop thinking of exercise as more of that self-improvement stuff and start thinking of it as rescue: private time, a tranquilizer (and energizer), an antidote for the poisons of modern life. Use exercise that way and you don't have to make yourself do it, you have to ration the dosage.

READINESS

Serious athletes don't get warm, they get "loose." They play around with the moves of their sport until they reach a shambling, tension-free kind of confidence that tells them they're ready for real effort. They don't pursue warmth, they pursue bounciness, elasticity, fluidity. The goal is to get the soft tissue pulled out to length, the joints lubricated through their ranges of motion, the synapses charged.

Getting loose reminds the nerves to remind the muscles just how to do that next demanding thing. Looseness is also a state of mind, much to be desired: tight minds make tight muscles, which make not only injuries but also tentative movements, turnovers, booted plays. Tight minds make bad athletes. Send me in, coach, I'm loose.

LETTING FLY

Athletic technique is always personal. We vary in dimensions from joint to joint, in angles and leverages of muscular attachment; we move these segments to our own internal rhythms. To the extent we can train the angles and leverages to work together better, to the degree the internal rhythms come to fit the physics of the task, we improve. We can only approach perfection, never arrive.

When we try to change our form, we tend to work too small; we're tentative. In athletic motion, what feels like a large correction is usually tiny. Full amplitude feels exaggerated, and we don't want to appear physical fools. To change your technique you have to act out, let fly, exaggerate. Once the change is grooved you can go back to subtleties.

WALLET PROTECTION, PART I

A lot of us modify our running programs on the basis of sketchy "scientific" information—and worse, on popular interpretation of it. Popular interpretation is, inevitably, a trip through the oversimplification machine. Nuance can be lost—or worse, added. Scientific language doesn't permit much speculation about meaning, even about application, leaving that to over-simplifying journalists like me.

We positively adore speculation; it is our life-blood. Believe me, if something about running is presented to you as "scientific," put your hand on your wallet.

GOING ORTHOPEDIC

One problem with middle-aged love affairs, a witty woman columnist writes, is the hesitation one feels in exposing one's sagging body to a lover's view. Not to worry about that, she says: he's probably on the verge of going orthopedic himself.

That term brought a hoot of rueful laughter from me: I've been going orthopedic more or less since I started running. Since I started exercising, really—by which I mean working my body just to work the body, as opposed to pursuing some specific sport or pastime.

That's a critical distinction. If you're playing a sport, the aches and pains that inevitably occur along the way seem entirely like accidents. They always surprise (and insult) you. If instead your attention is on what you're doing with your body, aches and pains seem more like an entirely natural development. They're almost to be expected, planned for, accommodated into your schedule. When you're using yourself hard—and enjoying it—overuse is never very far away. The older you get, of course, the nearer that threshold lies.

Going orthopedic doesn't necessarily mean suffering injury, it just means paying a little more attention to the signals that say that injury (let's call it orthopedism) is a possibility—especially if you continue this particular foolishness at this particular rate or intensity. It is the sure sense that in athletic activity you can at any point push over into pain, if not actual injury.

It's always there, but it isn't necessarily a bad thing. It helps guide our training; it also keeps us from being truly foolish. After all, it's much better to feel that if we push too hard we're going to have a sore Achilles tendon or even runner's knee than that if we push too hard we're going to have an infarction. Psychologically, the whole point of exercise seems to be to have something against which we can safely push. Eventually, orthopedism is what we push against.

Orthopedism is also that sense of self-preservation that younger athletes so spectacularly lack. Maybe when we're young the only things we can really push against are opponents, the rules of the game, the restrictions of the discipline. We can't push against ourselves because we don't have any limits, or can't conceive of them. That sense of invulnerability, which all of us at some point have felt, is the opposite of orthopedism. Maybe the great endurance athletes are the ones who early on conceive of themselves as having limits, and learn to work within—and against—those limits. They learn to manage them.

In a wonderful little essay called "Close to Zero," Harry Remde talks about the craftsman and craftsmanship, but he could just as well be talking about athletic training: "At every moment [the craftsman] works close to a boundary, an invisible wall that defines the path to the next moment, that moves ahead of him as he follows it, a wall that he never quite touches. . . . At each stroke of the tool he brings his work up to it. . . . His thoughts and movements are bounded by the wall. His emotion makes the nearness of the wall satisfying to him. When he has finished the movement, the wall moves beyond, establishing the further step. Again he moves close to it. The movements of the wall and the craftsman are nearly continuous, nearly the same."

GOING SYSTEMIC

Going orthopedic is falling over the edge into orthopedic injury, either from overuse or age, whichever comes first. Looking at the careers of some flash-in-the-pan road racers, I'm wondering if there isn't another, admittedly rarer but more serious threat to long and happy running. It might be called going systemic.

The fact is that a strange and mysterious affliction occasionally comes along and knocks an elite athlete out of contention—sometimes permanently: the Alberto Salazar phenomenon, so to speak, for that seemingly unbeatable marathoner whose career a couple of decades ago suddenly spiraled off into despair. Salazar was famous for two things: training more ferociously than anyone else, and racing the same way—driving himself on at least one occasion near the point of death. Then he "disappeared," dropping from contention, and was later diagnosed as having a blood disorder. Despite the best medical attention, he never regained his former levels of performance. Something similar happened to the runner Craig Virgin. Both of their systemic problems were purportedly cured, but their comebacks were then marred by orthopedic disruptions. If the blood doesn't get you, their bodies seemed to be telling them, the connective tissue will.

Maybe these elite athletes forget that their lofty status is in large part a genetic gift, and think that they can overwhelm any problem with hard work. It's fairly clear that gross over-training is the culprit, although the medical profession is at a loss for a clear explanation why. At the elite level, any runner is willing to train hard enough to hit the wall. There's an old bit of athletic paranoia about how at any given moment there is someone somewhere who is training when you're not. When your rest is disturbed by such thoughts, you're almost asking for a wipeout. When runners are willing to do enough work to destroy themselves, the winners are going to be the ones blessed with the genetic makeup that allows them to endure such training without breaking down. Maybe athletic skyrockets like Salazar are the ones who refuse to recognize that breakdown points always lie in wait.

Orthopedists in general—not just sports-medicine specialists—are finally beginning to see clearly how the mechanisms of overuse can work, and how almost inevitably they result in wear-and-tear injuries. But other physicians seem curiously reluctant to grasp that metabolic systems themselves might also suffer from sheer fatigue. Nevertheless, every four years several thousand athletes train themselves to a wire-thin edge, all reserves exhausted, and then

gather in a village somewhere. Invariably a substantial percentage of them come down with
what the press calls "Olympic flu." The really
silly thing about it is that it gets diagnosed by
journalists, not physicians.

TWO CULTURES

Traditionally, the popular sports in this country have been almost exclusively sprint-based.
Baseball, football, and basketball are all organized around speed, all played on venues whose
maximum dimensions can be covered on foot in
seconds, not minutes. Court games, stick-and-
ball games, always put a premium on quickness.
Strength and stamina help, of course, but the
very design of the competition measures speed
first. Even in track and field, the majority of the
events are the brief ones, which test fast-twitch
muscles and anaerobic energy systems above all
else. Endurance events in any sport have always
been for crazies. (I used to cover downhill skiing, a sprint sport if ever there was one. Slalom
coaches referred to cross-country ski racers as
"Nordic apes.")

The British scientist and novelist C. P. Snow

once proposed the unfortunate idea that modern society is divided into two cultures. Scientists will never understand men of letters, and vice versa; never the twain shall meet. Unfortunately, you can almost say that about sports: we have a fast-twitch culture and a slow-twitch culture. Let's not get into the argument about which one is really crazy.

FALLING

Maybe I shouldn't be telling this, but I fall down, while running, two or three times a year. Maybe four or five. In part this is because I am clumsy—or inattentive, same thing—and in part because I live in the Northeast, where winter running conditions are, well, complex and challenging, if not exactly awful. It isn't always a patch of ice that brings me down: I also slip on wet rocks or wet logs in the woods where I like to run, on slopes too steep for the speed I try to carry up or down them. I've even fallen down while running on wet grass.

Falls are more or less inescapable, I've come to realize, and the trick is not to mind it too much. Try to go down easily. I suppose one should practice, to ingrain the habit of accepting the inevitable. Football players, whose game is predicated on making each other fall down as much as possible, do practice, and the grace with which they tumble and slide can be breathtaking to watch. Not as breathtaking as doing it, though, since getting one's breath knocked out is one of physiology's least pleasant experiences.

Trying too hard to escape a fall can be a mistake. Sometimes it isn't the impact of the fall that hurts, it's the muscular wrench in trying to get your balance back before you actually fall. You can get hurt worse trying to keep from falling than from hitting the ground. I hate that. I also hate the insult, the momentary humiliation, that comes from losing my balance. It never fails to make me angry—at myself, of course, for not paying better attention.

In spite of all that I still like winter running best. The only real problem is overcoming inertia: getting suited up and out the door. I know perfectly well, from experience, that once I'm warmed up I'll have a fine time. If I just watch where I put my feet.

WHINING

Runners do a lot of, um, whining, and no-body, as the saying goes, likes a whiner. I'd like to claim for us some mitigating circumstances. This noxious habit springs from the impulse toward perfection, and therefore at least has a positive, if not always benign (and not necess-arily nonirritating), source.

It's the same impulse that starts most of us running in the first place: the urge to improve something—our capacity to manage stress, our slothful ways, our cardiovascular health.

ILIOTIBIAL BAND SYNDROME

There you are at a cocktail party, talking to an Attractive Member of the Opposite Sex (here-inafter AMOS). You lean one hand on a nearby wall. (Your other hand holds your drink.) You cross one leg over the other and sag your body toward the wall, grimacing slightly, or maybe groaning with pleasure. "Good Lord, what's wrong?" asks your AMOS, or target-of-opportu-nity. "Iliotibial band tightening up," you say. "Must have been that 15K I ran last weekend."

Perfect. I ran across the iliotibial band syndrome while flipping through an old running magazine, and saw its usefulness immediately: a hot new ailment, the In injury, the ache of the month. It's much better than the previous month's, plantar fasciitis.

Plantar fasciitis is an overuse injury to the sheet of tissue connecting the heel to the ball of the foot. Pound on it too much and it starts tightening up; unattended, it will start fatiguing, usually at the juncture with the heel. Without time to heal, it can tear or develop lumps of scar tissue or bone spurs. Stretching it out helps, but massage is better, even self-massage. You can do that at a cocktail party, but you have to sit down and take off a shoe, which is likely to interrupt conversation with your AMOS.

Besides, the trouble with plantar fasciitis is that even if you can get your AMOS to sit down and talk to you while you're massaging it, you can't really discuss what you're doing, because no one knows how to pronounce fasciitis. I heard someone give it a good try once, but the conversation immediately swerved off into political argument. The person to whom the sufferer was describing her plantar fasciitis thought she was talking about planetary fascism. He said the UN ought to deal with matters like that—which puzzled Ms. Plantar Fasciitis no end. Sort of put an end to the conversation right there.

The same thing happened when the beady eye of pop medicine fell on the psoas. The psoas is the large muscle that attaches the front of the lower spine across the pelvis to the thigh. You use it every stride, every time you swing your leg. It tightens up from overuse, and needs regular stretching to keep you from losing range of motion at the hip. You can stretch it at cocktail parties, too, if you don't mind looking a little silly. (Other runners will understand.) Lean one hand against a wall, as above, and—putting down your drink—grab your foot behind your back. Pull your foot upward, keeping straight at the waist and resisting at the knee so that the stretching force is transferred to the front of the pelvis. Feels good, doesn't it? Trouble is, when your AMOS asks what the hell you're doing and you say, "Stretching my psoas," your AMOS is likely to respond, "So as to what?" So as to look like a jerk?

No such problem with the old iliotibial band. This is the large sheet of tissue that connects the crest of the pelvis to the knee. It rubs against

the outside of the knee, and sometimes gets irri-
tated, causing pain in the hip or knee—or both.
Stretching helps, and you can stretch it out anytime you're standing. Best of all is that as mysterious, complicated, even heroic as it sounds,
anybody can say it with a little practice. Rolls
right off the tongue. If things really start click-
ing, you can even let your AMOS feel how tight
your iliotibial band is.

DANCING

Jacques d'Amboise is a former principal
dancer with the New York City Ballet and
founder of the National Dance Institute,
which teaches dance to schoolchildren in New
York and New Jersey. He has a very athletic
take on dancing. Our first memories, from the
very womb, are of rhythm and movement, he
says. "All babies begin their lives dancing. It's
in the rhythm of our breathing; it's in our
heartbeat. Dance is a means of participating
in time and space."

So is running. That's why it is so important
to us. That's what I can't understand about
those folks who are stubbornly nonphysical.

They thereby lose a magnificent chance to participate in time and space. How could they possibly pass up that? When full participation is only a dance, or a run, away? Running, after all, is only a dance that covers distance.

SHARPENING

Elite runners set out regularly to achieve a state of physical acuity they refer to as sharpness. To be sharp is to attain a kind of highly energized physiological clarity. It brings an improved quality of movement, of response, of mental and physical grasp. You achieve this state by tapering.

The taper is an attempt to supersaturate the body with recovery. You build up workout intensity to a peak well before the big day; then you cut down gradually, day by day, until you arrive at the meet well rested and in fine fettle.

The details can be extremely complex, but when it works you get into a wonderful state, one that can linger for a couple of weeks. You feel quick, alert, full of energy. You find yourself snapping awake early and hitting the floor running, on a roll with regard to much more than just your sport. Sharp.

II

SPRING

Now we really begin to run. Early spring always brings a restless itchiness: the weather keeps not-breaking and not-breaking, staying just slightly too miserable for all the other outdoor stuff we want to do. Might as well run run run.

Except for the blasted wind. If you've ever doubted that March is the windy month, try spending it in West Texas. There, March sets up a weather pattern that brings uninterrupted thirty-mph winds for about six weeks, rattling windows night and day, yanking doors out of people's hands, knocking hats off. I remember once talking about it with a large, gloomy old-timer as we stood watching tumbleweeds blow down the road. With a sigh he told me that before the spring winds stopped blowing he'd lose twenty pounds. Happened every year. Gets on your nerves.

That was in high desert, but seashores and mountains are windy places too. One of the discouragements of mountain-climbing is how windy the summits almost always are—just when you want to sit down and enjoy the serenity of all that space and distance. But then the wind always seems to get a vindictive joy out of opposing human-powered activity. It not only comes, invariably, from the wrong direction, but it'll even switch on you, through a complete 180 degrees, if you give up and decide to turn around. I can't remember a bicycle or canoe trip when this didn't happen. You start dreaming about how easy it's going to be when you come back the other way; you turn around; in about ten minutes it's in your face again, guaranteed.

Running, of course, is no different from other expeditions. When you're running, the wind drags and buffets extra energy out of you even when it's coming from behind. It also exacerbates the problem of management of body heat, taking too much heat away when you're headed into it, preventing you from dissipating as much heat as you need to when you're going with it.

In the northern temperate zone the wind blows most of the time either from the northwest or the southwest. Where I live now, in western Massachusetts, an occasional wind from the east will bring instant rain, but that's a rarity; the rest is dependably from the southwest or the northwest. In May the southwest wind brings the songbirds, waves of them arriving from Dixie whenever the thermometer achieves another upward spike. The rest of the year, however, what it brings is the miasmic atmospheric garbage from the urban megalopolis to the south. When the wind is from the northwest it is cleansing and clarifying, letting us breathe again. (In my imagination the Adirondacks scrub it clean, removing whatever gunk it picked up on its way across the Midwest.) Because I live in a rural area I've probably grown oversensitive to this change of air, but it's amazing how depressing it is when a spate of that southern air sets in, and how vivifying it is when it swings back around to the north.

I've never lived on a coast, except for a couple of stints on Manhattan Island. Then I never knew which way the wind was blowing.

BEGINNINGS

Let out of its stall, a horse will always run, indulging its natural urge toward liveliness after the stasis of the barn. It will take a quick turn of the pasture, settling into a trot, a jog, tossing its head, shuddering in pleasure at freedom. I defy any runner to witness such animal joy without smiling. It reminds us that we are physical creatures, too: we also have muscles, and the need to work them.

Joyful is not how it feels, though, when we resume running after a layoff. We feel so unspeakably heavy, our feet leaden, joints rebellious. Beginnings are when we have to wheedle and bargain with ourselves to continue. At that stage there doesn't seem anything natural about running. Of course the inactivity that detrained us was unnatural, too. *Sedentary* comes from the same Latin root as *sediment,* and that's how we feel: all silted up.

There are good reasons not to make a religion out of running, but one small leap of faith is required, whether it's to resume an interrupted running career or to get started in the first place. You have to believe in the training effect, the astonishing physiological principle that says the organism improves in response to stress. It's the principle that will eventually remove the lead from your feet, that will relubricate your joints. Every runner, every athlete, has experienced its gentle galvanization. Every one of us has come to know that if we are only steadfast, the training effect will rescue us from torpor and temporary discomfort.

On difficult days, when failed resolutions lie

all around us, it doesn't work well to run in order to lose weight, to improve our sex lives, to reduce our insurance premiums, even to get, or stay, in shape. Rationales are too hard to hang on to.

Instead, try to go running like a colt turned out of its stall into a spring pasture. Try to run for the running, just because it is one dependable thing that a physical being can do to shake off the dullness of the indoor hours and the diminishment of vigor that a long hard winter can foist upon us.

GRACE

Physical performance gets better—more beautiful was well as more productive—as it gets more efficient. Athletes and performing artists eventually learn to give up force for accuracy, for precision. Getting the physical task precisely right is not only the easiest way, and therefore the most forceful way, but the most beautiful way as well. It is the truest way, in the carpenter's sense of straight lines and proper alignments. It turns out to be the most effective and the most aesthetic way too.

It is when you attempt to lay something extra on top of the pure performance of the task that things go out of whack. That's when ego starts getting in the way of physics.

MECHANICS

There are two ways to think about the effects of work on the body. The more popular one is chemical in its approach; *aerobics* might be considered its shorthand code word. Aerobics simply means "oxygen-using," but the fitness movement has broadened the term to apply to most of the biochemical processes having to do with the exchange of energy. If you get interested enough in running to dig into its physiology, what you come across first is biochemistry: aerobic and anaerobic processes, lactic acid, blood composition, that sort of thing. Much of what we think of as "scientific" training —in the relatively new science of exercise physiology—comes out of this chemical investigation. If it hasn't quite revolutionized human performance (and that's arguable), it has at least provided a way of testing the older, more intuitive approaches to training, and discarding the less effective.

But there is also a mechanical aspect to running and its effect on the body. Unfortunately, biomechanics is even more of an upstart discipline than exercise physiology, in large part because it's harder to do science on the mechanical structures of the body. We still don't know, for instance, how muscle really works. We can explain the chemistry of the linkup but not the mechanics.

Muscle tissue is tough to study because it won't hold still. It's a problem with tissue. Our bodies are too squishy; when we try to work with them we suddenly discover we can't measure anything, can't hang markers, can't find our way into the sites without disrupting them. Can't find anything out. It's very hard to do science that way.

But we can think mechanically, about human movement. Strangely enough, we do so most effectively on the downside: when we're thinking about injury. When you're trying to figure out how something happened, or whether it's going to get worse, or how you're going to rehabilitate it, you're forced to consider the mechanical properties of your tissues and how they deal with the forces and angles generated by your running. It's a way of turning a downside into an upside. Once you start thinking mechanically, you're forced to think about how tissue works best. As you sort out those angles and attachment points and lines of force, you reinforce your understanding of efficiency— economy of movement—as the ultimate goal, the highest good, as far as running is concerned.

The more economical you can make your stride, the farther, faster, and safer you can run. A deeper understanding of the mechanics of running, in other words, can improve your performance—and, more important, your enjoyment of your performance—just as effectively as the more chemical approach.

WEAR-DATED

Note down the purchase date of your running shoes. Trying to make a pair of running shoes last too long is hard on your musculoskeletal system. Besides, if you find a pair that lasts an unusually long time—or an unusually short one—that's worth knowing next time you're ready to buy new shoes.

MADNESS

"March Madness," the annual NCAA basketball tournament, is upon us, filling the home screen with exuberant young athleticism. The TV name implies craziness, March hares, loony bursts of springtime energies, but where I live it's much too early for that. Hereabouts the sweet part of spring, when every day the outdoor world becomes a more delicious place in which to run, is still a few weeks away.

The basketball championships aren't about springtime anyway, they're about grinding the other team down. The tournament is a long, exhausting process, and the team that wins is usually the one that avoids injuries to key players or that has a deep bench. Coaches delight in "putting some hurt" on the opposition, and other athletic clichés. They watch for every telltale sign of weakness, for pressure points. If you catch your opponents hanging on their shorts at the free-throw line, you immediately call for a full-court press. You've got their tongues hanging out, now run 'em ragged.

I have a problem with this aspect of competition, very likely a hangover from the Boy Scouts or some other Victorian institution. When I was competing regularly, what I wanted—perhaps too idealistically—was to win on the basis of my own energies and skills. When psychology entered into it, something a little poisonous came into the contest. Trying to psych people out, searching for ways to make it more painful for the other fellow, took a little of the fun out of it. When your opponent is no longer capable of full response, it stops being a contest. "Take your best shot" is far from an empty challenge: it is exactly what you want the other fellow to do, just as it is what you want to do yourself.

Athletics doesn't have to be this way, of course. Your competitors, after all, are joined with you in an enterprise aimed at bringing out the best in you as well as themselves. Looked at in those terms, it is possible, the moment the finish line is crossed, to be swept with a feeling for your adversaries that's pretty close to love.

I've had that feeling myself, which is perhaps why something about the adversary stage bothers me. When I see my competitor begin to fade, I feel a little surge of selfish joy. Can't help it, but I don't like it; it is not ennobling; it is tainted somehow, corrupting. Competition lights a little fire in me that I would prefer not to have lit. It is rather like the impulse to steal, to be unfaithful. It is an occasion of sin. Makes me uneasy.

There is a problem, however, with this attempt at nobility. That psychology stuff can work two ways. I notice that the moment you begin embracing your competitors, on some level you start settling for second place. I like coming in second even less than I like seeing the other fellow drop out. Conundrums like this can drive you a little crazy, along about March.

CALLOUSNESS

A callus is a thickened patch of skin that builds up in response to steady wear. Runners get them on their feet, guitar pickers get them on their fingers, cyclists . . . wear shorts with chamois inserts.

If you have a lot of calluses—or are an insensitive clod—you are "calloused": hardened, armored, incapable of discriminating subtle feelings. If you aren't calloused enough, you're in danger of becoming a neurasthenic, hypersensitive to life's harder lessons and therefore at continual risk. Can't we find some healthy middle ground here somewhere?

TAKING A BREAK

Running is for now, training for later. Training is about increase, improvement; it is future-oriented, aimed at pushing back the edge of the envelope. Running is for the run itself.

It's only when you run for the running that you can hope to flow. It's worth a try now and then. You can't train all the time, you know.

PIECES

Interval work—breaking your workout into pieces—is the most powerful tool yet devised for improving physical performance. There are several reasons why this is so. Shorter work periods build up less lactic acid, allowing you to do more volume, or work at a higher intensity, with less accumulated fatigue. Interval training also lets you spend more time in recovery. The heart attains maximum stroke volume during recovery—and maximum improvement in aerobic capacity is achieved during those times when the heart is working at maximum stroke volume. More recovery time also reduces overuse injuries: the mechanical structures, the hard-used tendon and bone and ligament, have time to be resupplied with blood and nutrients. Tissues stay healthier. Both stress fractures and tendinitis are caused more by insufficient recovery time than by the trauma of the work itself.

When a work period goes on too long, concentration fades, attention lags, you forget to take vitally necessary breaks. If the job is to get yourself, or your workload, from Point A to Point B in the quickest way possible, then the unbroken stint is the answer. But if quality rather than quantity is the aim, then doing the work in pieces may be much more efficient. And training that way will leave you in much better shape for the next time you need to go from A to B in an unbroken stint.

WORLD PEACE

Regular aerobic exercise has been shown to decrease aggression and lessen irritability—at least in laboratory rats. Rats on an exercise program fight less frequently and less violently than sedentary rats—but defend their turf more effectively. Moreover, hostile responses to teasing, used to measure irritability, are reduced by as much as eighty percent in the rats that have been given access to exercise. Personally, I've noticed the same tendency in myself.

GRAVITY

Some runners hate hills, some don't—but not hating hills doesn't mean you actually have to love them, does it?

It is gravity that gets you down, of course, that tireless magnetism of the earth itself. We spend our lifetimes dealing with it, adjusting to it, accommodating it, and ought to be able to manage it perfectly well. But along comes the gentlest of inclines, and we discover we can't. Hills are gravity-intensifiers.

Even on the flat, though, it is gravity as much as distance that we're struggling against. You have to get the body weight up—free, momentarily, of the friction of the ground—before you can move it forward. (Otherwise you'd wear off your feet.) Lifting the body requires more energy than driving it forward. Good marathoners know this well, which is why they hone their running style in the direction of the shuffle rather than the bound; they may bounce around all over the place in training, building strength, but when race day comes and energy becomes precious, they come down to earth.

Most training is aimed at improving our resistance to gravity's force. We dream of training ourselves so well that gravity stops being a burdensome load and becomes merely the grounding from which we work—defining, in a sense, what it is our muscle works against. Get strong enough and gravity should just be the force that keeps us stable, that gives us a point of departure. Until, that is, another hill comes along.

We also use training to resist gravity's ravages, over time, to our physical structure, although we don't think of it this way very often. Actually, gravity itself is a training force, gradually reshaping—downward—our mutable human bodies. All those bodywork schemes, yoga and Rolfing and the Alexander Technique and all the rest, always tell you to imagine that a string is tied to the top of your skull, pulling you upwards. Live that way, we are told; get taller. Resist.

If this sounds too much like work, why not

just escape for a while? Unfortunately, gravity-free time, available in space flight, turns out to be no solution either. When gravity's power is reduced, the astronauts have to supply a substitute for it to maintain health: artificial loading, aka exercise. Otherwise the body starts training for zero gravity, which is a maladaptation if you come back down to earth. Weightlessness will detrain you even faster than bed rest.

Fortunately, if you regularly overload the physical body—with gravity or anything else—it will respond by growing stronger. And it's not how heavy the body you're moving around, but what percentage of your capacity is being used. Adding strength is the same as reducing gravity.

Then a hill comes along and increases it again. Come to think of it, if aging is an effect of gravity on the body, then hills, you might say, accelerate aging. Hills make you older. But that's something runners have always known.

DEEP RECREATION

Perhaps we can more easily take care of the heart if we simply forget about it and run to relieve stress instead. That might do more for the heart and blood pressure even than periodically driving the heart rate up and then letting it recover, which is the strictly physiological view of aerobic exercise.

Actually, it's one of those wonderful can't-lose situations, isn't it? Physiology says that the exercise will help the heart anyway. If you want to distract yourself with thoughts of psychological gain, what could be wrong with that?

THE HEART OF A RUNNER

A low resting heart rate is generally regarded as the hallmark of fitness. A well-trained heart pumps more blood with each stroke, accomplishing more work with less energy expenditure. It has more time to rest between beats, an unmitigated good. People who are very fit often have resting heart rates in the low fifties, sometimes even the forties. Anything below sixty beats per minute is lodged in my mind, anyway, as a kind of virtue, something akin to high moral character. It means that you've done your work.

INHALE, EXHALE

The other day I found myself thinking of breathing out—exhaling—as a kind of bellows blowing on the coals of life. That was the image that came to me, anyway: that taking in air fuels the lungs, the heart, the muscles, but letting it out again is what makes the inner fire glow brightly.

I suppose this fanciful image comes from thinking about the respiratory drive. I hadn't realized it, but I think of the inhale part as purest need, blind acquisition, and the exhale part as relief. When you're breathing hard, the letting go of air seems more important than the cramming in.

LENGTHENING

We use muscle to run, of course, but it isn't muscle that should be the cause of our concern, it's connective tissue. That's the box the muscle comes in, the stuff that holds the muscle together, that transmits into movement the force the muscle generates. If muscle is the engine, connective tissue is the transmission, differential, suspension system, wheels, and tires: the means of getting power to the road. And connective tissue, much more than muscle (or body fluid or nerve), is the part that ages.

Therein lies a perfect metaphor for what exercise actually should be about: holding off the gradual shrinkage not only of the length of the hamstrings but also of other physical capabilities. All of the deleterious results of inactivity, otherwise known as "aging," have to do with a kind of shortening—of energy supplies, of the time before fatigue sets in, of the capacity to make a meaningful effort—as well as of tissue length. That's the way aging works: it simply reels us in. Movement is the only way we have of resisting.

ANTIFREEZE

We acclimate to heat after five to twelve days of working out in it. Thus we should be able to overdress for the first week or so of warm-weather running in the spring and take care of the matter.

We do not acclimate physically to cold, but a certain amount of psychological acclimation may be necessary. This may be what motivates

JOHN JEROME

the people who insist on running in shorts and singlets long after everyone else has gone to full-length gear, who specialize in running in the least possible clothing—or who run in various other kinds of extremes.

Their motivation is clearly different from the one that leads people to take off their shirts at snowy football games, although I'm not sure how. Those guys (you wouldn't see women doing that, now, would you?) are simply overdosed on antifreeze.

THE QUIET BODY

One of the most disquieting physical moments I've ever had came after an all-out sprint to the finish, when I was simultaneously gasping for air and choking with thirst. I made the mistake of taking a big mouthful of water before I'd caught my breath—and thought I was going to suffocate before I could get the water swallowed. The conflicting demands for replenishment of air and water were knocking me back and forth like the Ping-Pong ball behind the playroom door.

That's the noisy body talking, the one that

clamors and shouts, that you can't ignore if you try. It's the obstreperous lump of meat, bone, and nerve endings that you push around every day—or that pushes you around every day. People always say you have to listen to your body, but there's really no need to listen to that one at all. It does all the talking.

The body you do have to listen to is the quiet one inside. That's the one that sits there observing your bad habits (but not necessarily taking part in them), often as not muttering under its breath. (Oh what a fool inhabits me, I imagine mine saying.)

The quiet body is the one that stretches when you arise from a period of stasis, for example, because it knows that the longer (in length) you are, the longer (in time) you can go on; that the longer you are, the longer you live; that only when all of your soft parts are pulled out to their optimum operating length are you really ready to do anything.

The quiet body is in charge of all your set points: not just the one that maintains your weight but the ones for respiration and sleep and sex and everything else. The quiet body is stubborn and slow, slow to move (but not necessarily slow to react, if you've done the training).

It is the body that knows when to quit and when not to start, in everything from exercise sessions to bedtime snacks. But you can seldom hear it for the noisy one.

You may have to motivate the quiet body, to apply a little conscious direction to get it moving —but it, too, is mutable, and it has great momentum. That's the thing that nobody says clearly enough about exercise: how it gets things humming, gets the energy level up, the systems working, everything cooking. Just do that part and the quiet body will start carrying this new energy and momentum over into your daily life—whether you're listening to it or not. You'll find yourself doing things with a little more flair, more pizzazz, more reward. And all you have to do to reap these rewards is give a little kick to the momentum wheel now and then.

PANACEAS

"There's no evidence that exercise prevents, retards, or cures coronary disease, or any other disease, for that matter," said the late Dr. George Sheehan, the New Jersey cardiologist who was one of running's more eloquent spokesmen. "The case for exercise is that it makes you fit. Exercise physiology is the science of human performance. It really has nothing to do with pathology."

THE W-WORD

Running, you realize, is work.

Well, maybe it's not as bad as it sounds. After all, lifting a glass of champagne to your lips is also work, in the physiological sense. So is kissing your sweetie pie.

One definition of work is force times distance resulting in motion, but you might have a little trouble digging that out of *Webster's Third:* "the transference that is produced by the motion of the point of application of a force . . . and is measured by multiplying the force and the displacement of its point of application in the line of action." Sounds like work to me, says this typist, applying force to the keys. Anyway, running definitely qualifies as work, sometimes.

In fact, work physiology is the proper name of the wonderful young science that has sprung up around running (and all other athletic endeavors), although it is more commonly called things like exercise science, and the halls where its secrets are pursued are usually known as human-performance laboratories. "Human" is perhaps misleading; work in this sense is the application of effort, and is the same (and has exactly the same science to it) whether it is being applied by man, beast, or insect. Ultra-marathoner Bernd Heinrich has written a wonderful book, *Bumblebee Economics,* about that last category. There is an enormous amount to learn about work.

It doesn't necessarily have to be unpleasant duty, either (see sweetie pie, above). The problem with work is mostly that it's always gotten a bad press, ever since we got kicked out of Eden. We've gotten it mixed up with labor; that's the miserable part.

I don't like unpleasant work any more than the next person, and I'd be the first to admit that running can turn into that at any time. When it does, I find that thinking about the science of it can remove some of the sting. When a run begins to turn laborious on me, I try to find some physiological aspect of the task to think about as a device for dissociating from the discomfort. I like to conjure up the growing of new capillaries (and the reopening of old, abandoned ones), the laying down of great, free-flowing vascular beds habituated to high levels of use. I envision the firming up and the stripping down of the muscle cells, those slim red bundles of possibility, honed by steady work in the direction of endurance.

No doubt these images are faulty. I am no scientist, and surely understand the processes imperfectly. That's okay: the mental pictures still provide solid entertainment, on those occasions when I'd rather not think about how tired I'm getting, or how my feet are starting to hurt. And entertainment is important, of course, because running is also play. When I am not succeeding in keeping it that way, I try to watch kids, dogs, animals that run and birds that fly for the fun of it; creatures that do work for play, which is the best definition I know of athletics.

Personally, I find that the nature of the goal has a lot to do with holding on to that attitude. The times when running really turns into work are those when the only reason I'm running is to get somewhere else more quickly. When it's play, though, I lose all interest in arriving at my destination.

CHECK IT OUT

I'm always struck by how meticulously top-level athletes warm up. This shouldn't surprise, considering how much depends on careful maintenance of their physical plants. Still, the thoroughness of their preparation always impresses me. (And the attitude, the very air: it seems to be important to cool out while you're warming up, doesn't it?) The militaristic drills of our school days have long since given way to introspective stretching, to the jiggling, floppy-jointed, desultory jog. You see bursts of real effort now and then, but most warm-up time seems devoted to a kind of leisurely checking-out—of hamstrings, groins, throwing arms. Among serious athletes there are no nonparticipants in this enterprise.

RELAXATIONS

Rest time between muscular contractions is enormously important in endurance sports. Most great distance runners say they became successful when they learned to relax while they were racing. Sounds implausible, but I assume they mean they relax every possible muscle for every possible microsecond it is not in actual use. They don't waste energy overcontrolling, carrying excess tension, straining at the pace with anything except what drives them down the road.

GOING OUTDOORS

I've never done my running indoors. A lot of people do, feeling forced to by some combination of weather and unfortunate location. They may be missing a bet. I'd rather go for a bad run in real weather than a good one in no weather at all, the weather, every day, having become one of the larger parts of the experience.

By "weather" I mean what the earth is doing that day with its atmosphere and its physics, with its growing season and its multitude of life cycles. That for me has become almost the most important part of the deal.

Running is not only the thing that gets me off my duff, it is also the thing that dependably gets me out of the house. In recent years I've come to realize that the more of the outdoors I get, the more I want. That alone—that growing appetite for being out in the natural world—is a debt to running that I can never repay.

CUTTING APEXES

The bulk of my running takes place on old logging roads that wind through New England woods. The twistiness of the roads is in search of the most nearly level path, of course. Usually I am accompanied by two dogs, who've come along on my daily runs for years. They're not so picky about the route: on some of the more egregious loops and swerves they simply cut across. They've taken these shortcuts so often they've worn their own paths, little doggy highways from one part of my route to the next. They prefer to cut the apexes.

The New York Marathon finishes in Central Park, the last few miles following a similarly tortuous road. Some runners, in these closing stages, are very conscious of apexes, carefully crossing back and forth from one curb to the other in search of the shortest route home. Others seem to pay no attention to apexes at all, and as a result run a longer distance.

Knowledgeable commentators pick this up, and soon have TV viewers straining along with the runners, trying to think them over to the shortest route. It's hard to visualize how critical these shortcuts are, even when you're out there running them—but think about the staggered starts in 200-meter and 400-meter track races. Those events demonstrate much more vividly than a marathon what a substantial difference there can be in hugging the curve.

Sometimes hugging the curve is, surprisingly, not the fastest way. In automobile road racing, in a succession of curves, the line that lets you out at the end with the fastest exit speed can be a tricky thing to find, particularly when there are curves in the middle with a decreasing radius or two thrown in. Some fancy physics is required. Ski racers also spend a lot of time working on line, although they don't talk about it as obsessively as motor racers. That may be because in a slalom race the turns come along about one every second, which doesn't give a whole lot of time for deliberating over the fine points.

Ski racers also have vertical curves to deal with, in the humps and bumps and fallaway sections of the course. They clip those apexes by prejumping the bumps, so they aren't thrown into the air where they lose speed. (Skis slide faster than they fly.) Cross-country runners have similar if less dramatic vertical curves to deal with. So do hurdlers. You'll often see steeplechasers step up onto the hurdle; if they could leap it cleanly—and thus not lift their entire body weight and then have to let it down again—they'd save time, of course. But in the closing stages of a 3000-meter race, who has the strength?

Questions of strength or energy further complicate the matter. Runners know very well that the fastest way is to maintain speed, rather than to burn off excess energy by decelerating and accelerating again. That's much more exhausting than simply going with the flow.

This all sounds very complicated, doesn't it? So how come even my dogs can figure it out?

IT'S THE LAW

One characteristic that all forms of athletics have in common is that they deal with physical laws—acceleration, deceleration, momentum and mass, vectors of force, the production and application of energy, the dissipation of heat. Knocking the ball out of the ballpark or chipping it out of a sand trap is a problem in practical physics; so is moving the human form 26.2 miles on foot or in a wheelchair faster than anyone else in the race. Whatever the discipline, an athlete is in the business of making judgments about, and applying, those physical laws in real time. The winner is the individual whose judgments and applications are most accurate. In this sense the ultimate athletic attribute isn't endurance, speed, strength, agility—or guts or heart—but accuracy. The best athlete is the one who gets the best reading from the world about what is required to solve the problem in physics that his particular athletic problem poses—and then comes up with the best approximation of that solution.

One set of athletic problems may have more appeal to you or me than the next, but at some level they all involve the same basic laws. And since at the highest levels a lot of very talented individuals are trying hard to solve them, success is going to represent excellence. I'm not sure that excellence in the solving of one set of physical problems is greater than excellence in the solving of another. The ones who achieve it all look great to me.

April runners often have to sell themselves the weather. It is weather, after all, that you're going to be running through, and that song about the showers and the flowers wouldn't have been written if April meteorology didn't have a certain undependable element to it. In the advertising business they used to talk about the Unique Selling Proposition, the one thing about the product that none of its competitors can claim. What we have to do is find the USP for April weather.

To stay comfortable while running in April, for example, you may have to resort to foul-weather gear. The idea of foul weather is an interesting one. *Foul* comes from the Latin word meaning "to stink." (It ain't the weather that stinks, of course, but the stuff we're putting into it.) The term has been around a lot longer than TV weathermen, but it represents the kind of thinking that those elegantly coiffured prognosticators like to foist off on us. They're the ones to whom nice is a nullity, for whom a mild, bright, sunny day is weather-less. For there to be weather there has to be action, drama—and, preferably, unpleasantness:

a discomfort factor, a reason not to go out.

So okay, we're not going to get the USP that April running requires from a television set. The thing is, throughout most of human history we lived and worked outdoors. We only really came indoors in the last few hundred years. Indoor thinking is different from outdoor thinking. Indoor thinking is likely to have you believing in what the weathermen say. If you're going to enjoy running in April, you have to take your thinking outdoors.

DISSOCIATION

One thing that distinguishes elite runners is their disdain for dissociation. The stars monitor their physiological state; we plodders pull any trick we can to take our minds off our growing fatigue. A principle is implied: if you want to improve as a runner, you will do so to the degree that you learn to pay attention to your body as you are using it.

PROPRIOCEPTION

Science is the business of driving cause into a corner. It is awash in wonderful mysteries. One of the lovelier ones is how the senses actually work. Scientists have no problem getting from light waves to rods and cones to the optic nerve and thence to the brain. But when it comes to the final transaction—the one that turns the electric signals back into a visual image in your mind—no explanations exist. "The eye acts as a transducer for the specific purpose of converting light energies to the electrical energies associated with the nerve impulse," says my physiology book. Fine. Now how do we get from information to experience?

I'm thinking about this because I've been trying to get my mind around proprioception, that wonderful sense that gives us the freedom to use all the other senses. The proprioceptors are the nerve endings embedded throughout the muscle, tendons, and joints that read and report on body position and the relation of body parts, on movement, loading, and acceleration, even on the rate of increase or decrease of acceleration. The nerve endings that pick up all this information are mechanoreceptors, fired not by light or sound waves or aromatic molecules but by actual physical displacement (movement) or would-be displacement (force). They send the information to both conscious and unconscious levels of the central nervous system. At the conscious level this information informs our volitional actions; at the unconscious level it initiates and controls our muscular reflexes.

Proprioceptors are the neural devices that perceive, weigh, and judge whatever we do with our bodies, from running a marathon to tying trout flies. They tell us where we are and what we're doing as we are doing it, and thus are our connection to the present tense of physical action. They are the junction between physics and physiology, the internal rigging that locates our body in time and space, the interior map of the body that redrafts itself with every move we make.

Some of us get very good with our proprioceptors. Those who do are frequently called athletes—or performers. Playing a violin concerto, for example, is one of the most dazzling demonstrations of proprioceptive capability you'll see.

Those of us who don't become good at proprioception are usually called spectators.

Science can explain a lot about proprioception, but not, in the end, how anyone can play a violin concerto. It is too complicated; too much information is processed too rapidly. This reminds me of an essay by the late Lewis Thomas called "On Embryology." He speaks of the unknown process that at some point switches on a single cell so it can grow into an entire brain. "All the information needed for learning to read and write, playing the piano, arguing before senatorial subcommittees, walking across a street through traffic, or the marvelous human act of putting out one hand and leaning against a tree, is contained in that first cell," says Thomas.

"No one has the ghost of an idea how this works," he continues, "and nothing else in life can ever be so puzzling. If anyone does succeed in explaining it, within my lifetime, I will charter a skywriting airplane, maybe a whole fleet of them, and send them aloft to write one great exclamation point after another, around the whole sky, until all my money runs out."

KETTLES AND POTS

One of the sporting world's most distressing characteristics is the propensity of certain "sportsmen"—including runners—to consider their own chosen excesses a measure of good taste and intelligence, and everyone else's, in the immense range of enthusiasms and activities that fall under the loose rubric of sport, to be idiotic. This is hardly fair—and fairness is what sports are supposed to be about, isn't it? After all, these sports and games are nothing more than the restless ways we use our energy to maintain our health, our sanity, and our ability to cope. There's no real point, is there, in all us pots calling those other kettles black?

FUNCTIONALITY

The other day I heard a young person complaining about getting sore from playing softball, and couldn't resist teasing him. Yeah, I said, and it'll never get any better. The older you get, the sorer it's going to make you. Then —realizing that I was taking unnecessary glee from this fact, not to mention from the youngster's discomfort—I tried to soften the message. It's okay, though, I said. That's really the only bad thing about aging. Loss of function is the part that hurts; everything else about getting older is terrific.

First things first. Whatever your age, hang

on to your functions. Added to all the other reasons for running is this one: remaining physically active is the only technique we have for doing that.

MOODS, PART I

It's been one of those days, and I start my run in a lousy mood. By the time I'm warmed up my mind has wandered off into the usual junk, all those exigencies of everyday life: money, health, family, career. The anxieties of the future, predictably enough, and the regrets of the past—not very fruitful things to think about, but unavoidable somehow. The next time I fill out an application I plan to list my occupation as "Worry."

I am decidedly unambitious, determined to do nothing more than work muscles and lungs. Move my blood, clean the system out a bit; that's all I'm after, I swear it. Goal enough— and before long that, mercifully, is taking up most of my attention. At least for a little while I forget to spend time on all that regrettable-past and anxiety-filled-future business. I venture for a small distance across the surface of the earth, and enjoy thinking about that, enjoy being on the planet. That's always a mood-changer.

VIRTUAL REALITIES

As the nay-sayers are always pointing out, running as a sport is over with, done for. Never mind the soaring entry numbers at marathons and 10Ks, we've obviously gone on to other things. We're out there blade-skating and kite-skiing and parachuting off office buildings to get our ya-yas. The human attention span is dwindling as fast as the twentieth century is drawing to a close, and if it ain't on MTV—or better yet, in a fifteen-second commercial containing at least forty-five jump cuts—it doesn't exist. Besides which if it can't be done on a video screen, it isn't going to make it past the year 2000 anyway.

Get with it, runners, or get left behind. We're as anachronistic as wooden sailing ships. We are retros, Luddites, techno-dullards, blue-footed boobies of the information age, and we're about to be left completely behind by the virtual-reality folks. They're quick to point out that there are a lot of easier ways to do what we do than to get out there on an actual road with our actual, heavy, burdensome bodies.

We're just the saps who actually like to get sweaty, who even enjoy making ourselves tired: who have this stubborn predilection for Actual Reality. (Now there is a concept for you. Something like acoustic guitar, isn't it? Or whole milk?) We're going to be left in the dust, all alone, grinding along on our weary legs, plodding up hill and down, dragging our unwieldy flesh along over actual, five-thousand-two-hundred-and-eighty-foot miles. One after another, until we are all tired out. And won't that be just the ticket? Won't that be nice?

TOLERATION

The object of the game in racing is to find the pace that you can just hold, that you think is going to kill you but that doesn't—quite.

This is a species of self-torture that makes nonexercisers mumble the word "sick," but I don't think it is. We human beings commit ourselves to many nonathletic enterprises that require us to spend time at a barely bearable pace. For some of us, working under fluorescent lights in tall office buildings at jobs we don't like certainly qualifies. There are marriages of which the same can be said. There is no shortage of nonathletic things to do that require hanging on and hanging on, at the teetering edge of the intolerable. Heck, I've known people who party that way. So running yourself out to the edge and back doesn't seem so sick after all.

GOOD NEWS, BAD NEWS

As you become more skilled as a runner you get more efficient biomechanically; improve your muscles' capacity to convert fuel into energy and you get more efficient biochemically. Reduce your body weight and less energy is needed to get you down the road; convert fat into lean muscle and you burn more calories sitting still. It would be insidious if it weren't all so beneficial.

The temptation is to think you'll get in good enough shape to make the workouts easier. The difficult lesson is that that's not the point. The only part that stays the same—that you must keep the same—is how hard the workouts are.

THE SUIT OF LEAD

Fatigue is a lead suit, a layer of physical heaviness that drags you down, while nagging you with the fantasy of what running might be like without it. It whispers in your ear—with the persistence of two million years of evolution behind it—"Rest. Now."

Ignore it. The comforts, in the end, outweigh the discomfort, which is a net gain. Continue.

RHYTHMICS

One good reason for a deliberate, careful warm-up is to establish a rhythm to your workout. You want to warm up enough to get everything not just moving well but slightly tired, pushed gently into the first fringe of fatigue. You want to burn off the uppermost layer of nervous energy. Then stop for a brief rest until the surge of recovery begins to set in, and start the hard part of your workout on the crest of that surge. If you don't, if you attempt to bull your way right on through the first slump of fatigue, your workout gets uncomfortable early on, which is discouraging. It will take longer to get everything balanced out so that you're perking along at a steady state.

The idea is to put in your effort when fatigue ebbs, recover while it is peaking. Start your workout that way and you improve your chances of evening out the peaks and valleys to come. You, rather than your laggardly physical responses, are in charge of rhythm.

That's what interval training is really about, although the experts usually don't present it that way. The idea is to train the recovery processes as well as the energy-production processes. Intervals take the level of effort a little farther, a little more quickly, then ease off a little earlier. Your systems learn to recover faster, to smooth out the blips. Steady aerobic work gently pulls the systems along; intervals push them around aggressively. Trained that way, the systems learn to widen the range of their response.

It's impossible to guess how many physical rhythms are at work. A beat turns into a hum when it gets too rapid; a pause of more than about ten seconds turns a beat into an event, at least to our consciousness. But our bodies can recognize, and make good use of, frequencies ranging from the split second to at least the annual. We're always being told to follow a hard-day, easy-day schedule, which is certainly rhythmic. Most of us arrive at a weekly program that works for us, and however its days are arranged, it will assuredly be rhythmic. We work for rhythmicity even in our running strides. There are plenty of other rhythms to be experimented with. Get more rhythmic in any aspect of your training and you'll run better.

THE INTERIOR LIFE

A friend of mine claims to have no interior life whatsoever—yet he runs marathons. I have trouble believing that anyone who runs does not have an interior life.

From the very first day I went running, I have used it as a mechanism for gaining access to my inner regions. I zone out. My body may be running a dogged three-mile loop that is as familiar as the inside of my mouth, but my conscious attention is a million miles away, circling Betelgeuse. It's a large part of why I run.

What I'm calling an interior life, others might refer to as stress relief, which I happen to think is running's major contribution to modern society. And the great thing about running is that the stress relief is there no matter how you go at it. It makes absolutely no difference to the body whether you run for exterior or interior purposes.

MAINTENANCE

When it comes to our physiology, we seem to think we're going to be allowed to skip the tedious details of maintenance. It's very American. We're in a hurry; we're looking for the physiological equivalent of that legendary big old domestic station wagon, the one that just sits there in the driveway waiting for you to start it up cold and drive it across the continent. Without even checking the air in the tires.

I've always claimed that whoever said there's no free lunch was not a runner. Just look: we increase energy by spending it. We relieve stress (on the nerves) by deliberately increasing stress (on the body). That's all free. But the warm-up is one place where no free lunch is available. You have to take the time to get the body ready to go. Otherwise you're asking for trouble.

ADVERSARIES

Recreational running is supposed to be non-adversarial. It's a sweet idea, and it even happens, on those rare days when everything flows, when muscles are silken and joints buttery, when energy supplies outlast the distance. But most of us, most of the time, have to have something to push against, on even the most cursory and ordinary runs. Fortunately for runners, there is never a shortage of adversaries: time, distance, the weather, the road, fatigue, the crest of the next hill.

STRIDE LENGTH

Older runners who maintain both volume and intensity of training also maintain such traditional measurements of fitness as maximum oxygen uptake. Despite the fact that they hang on to the measurements, however, their racing times gradually deteriorate. Aging racers slow down. Science has now finally come up with a reason: stride length. With training we maintain our turnover pretty well, the lab guys say, but our stride gradually closes up.

Stride length is another term for range of motion. Hairs can be split about active versus passive range of motion, but if you're not reaching out as far as you used to with your lead leg, something is keeping you from doing so. Some physical structure is in the way, either in the joint or in the musculotendinous tissue that links the bones. If it's in the joint, it's arthritis or injury, and that's another matter. If it's a shortening of the muscle and connective tissue, it is reversible with stretching. Stay loose and go fast, oldsters.

BALLISTICS

One of the few things that conventional stretching programs generally agree about is that ballistic stretching is not a good idea. *Ballistic* means stretching with momentum, as when you swing or "throw" a body part against its limits of motion. Bobbing down to touch your toes is a ballistic stretch. Before the exercise scientists got hold of it, ballistic stretching used to be a major part of calisthenics. (Remember them?)

Science is pretty vague when it comes to

stretching, but as far as I can figure, the ballistic version is now regarded as dangerous because the stretching force comes from deceleration: from stopping the motion. This means the tension is taken up at the narrow muscle ends, or muscle-tendon junctures, where there is not as much strength or elasticity.

Stopping a motion requires an eccentric contraction, in which force is generated not to shorten the muscle but to resist its lengthening. Eccentric contractions are the ones that put the most strain on the musculotendinous system, that do the most damage. So ballistic stretching is likely to make you sorer than the slow, gentle kind. It can allow you to hurt yourself. And we're not in this to hurt ourselves, right?

Except that if you don't do at least some training that is ballistic in nature, the muscles and tendons get no preparation for the stopping of motion. Then when you get into real-life situations where you need that capacity, when you need to take limbs abruptly to the limit of their range of motion, you don't have the strength to avoid getting hurt. So you might be safer in the long run to approach this problem from a training rather than a stretching point of view.

I'd think it worthwhile for us straight-ahead runners to spend some training time on these eccentricities. Certainly we do enough training of the usual concentric kind. Concentric contractions, after all, provide the muscle power we use to drive ourselves forward, to get up to speed: to accomplish things and to put the drive in our lives.

I find it an irresistible metaphor. Concentric contractions are the onward-and-upward part; eccentric contractions are the ones we use to bring ourselves back down again. And we are by nature such upward-striving creatures that it's the coming down again that we are seldom prepared for.

There's a kind of poetic justice, I think, in the fact that slowing down and stopping is the hard part. Not to overstretch the image, but the truth is that for every concentric contraction there has to be an eccentric one; and it is only by devoting as much attention to the seemingly unproductive, negative side of the equation that we maintain balance. Balance, surely, is the key. The highest levels of performance are always the product of a balanced effort.

BRAINS

Being an athlete does not necessarily mean being a dumb jock. Athletes are only people trying to get the most out of themselves. That's a cerebral enterprise if you go at it right, no matter how much muscle it takes.

TAKING YOUR TIME

More athletic moves go bad because they're launched too early than because they're too late. As a canny old pro once told me, you have to have the confidence to take the time. The complexity of this athletic truth grows on me daily.

III

SUMMER

BUGS

Summer running means bugs. I've had my problems dealing with the little devils. I guess it says something about how fast—or slow—I'm running. I outrun mosquitoes, blackflies, and biting gnats, but deerflies catch up with me and bite me on the run. I've never run into a problem with bees and wasps; if I did, I suspect they'd improve my interval times.

TOUCH

Inveigled on a summer afternoon into a casual game of touch football, I spend a giggling half-hour running buttonhooks and fly patterns. Twenty-four hours later I am sitting on one buttock, the other too tender to touch the seat cushion. No, not a catastrophic injury, just the focal point of my general, overall, ordinary delayed-onset soreness, the curse of the weekend athlete. The insult that is added to this injury is that the conditioning gained from my daily run didn't seem to help. I wince not only at my generalized crippling but also at the tired old lesson repeated one more time: sprinting and pacing are different. They use different muscles—or use the same muscles in different ways. Athletic training is specific. Always.

Will I never learn? I do this about once a year, not always at touch football: softball, badminton, or any other stop-and-start game will do the same damage. Traditionally, it happens in the context of a large picnic—you know, everyone feeling lively and having a great time outdoors, and maybe a beer or two along the way. The totally unserious game springs up spontaneously, just another way to have fun, get out and jump around on the grass and laugh a lot. That means sudden starts and bursts of speed, fakes, sharp cuts: not the sort of thing you do on a daily run. Bare feet and calves are worked hard, and midthigh to rib cage worked harder yet. Each time I swear, during the inevitable recuperation period, to be smarter next time. I forget. Next summer or fall I'll do it again, the thumbscrews of aging grown one year tighter.

My memory is short because my mental image of running is as a continuum, a progression. It's all locomotion, or somehow ought to be, from the pokiest jog—or slow walk—right on through the drop-dead, flat-out sprint. That image isn't entirely wrong: whatever the pace, we do use the same basic muscles to move our legs, stabilize our feet, maintain our moving balance, drive us forward. But every change of pace changes the loadings, changes the emphasis. Distance running gets your feet in fairly good shape for sprinting, for example, but doesn't do much for buttocks and upper thighs. Side loadings, or any other deviations from a straight line and an even pace, generate angles of tension that call into play muscles, and particularly their attachments, that at an aerobic pace are required to do nothing more than perk along at idle. The quicker you try to make those moves, the harder you yank on the attachment points. The next day you get an anatomy lesson in pain, a stern lecture in the biomechanics of athletics.

The lecture tells me that to avoid future agonies, I'd have to put in training at every level of the continuum. Who's got time for that? I'll have to settle for staying in shape for the utterly reliable pleasures of my daily run. And then when another one of those determinedly silly games seduces me into athletic foolishness, I'll go ahead and pay the price. I can always use the refresher course in anatomy.

SO WHAT?

Call it running's first cocktail fact: slow-twitch muscle fiber is used for endurance work, fast-twitch muscle for sprinting. The ratio of slow- to fast-twitch fibers in the muscle is genetically determined. Find out which predominate in your musculature and you know whether to become a sprinter or a distance runner. (A muscle biopsy is required.) No sense wasting time trying to overcome God-given genetic makeup. Or at least that was the gospel thirty years ago, when muscle-fiber typing burst on the scene.

A couple of decades of further research have not quite abolished that simple fast-twitch/slow-twitch dualism, but have complicated it nearly out of sight. At least one more type of fiber, or maybe five or six more, has been discovered. You can't change the type; what you can do is train both types—or all three, or all six—to be as good as possible at what you want them to do, whether it's distance running, sprinting, or playing hopscotch. If you want to be an elite athlete, knowing your muscle-fiber type might help you hone in on the events for which you're genetically suited. It won't change how hard you'll have to work, or how much fun you'll have trying to improve.

Maybe this should be put another way: if you're more interested in winning than in what it is you're winning at, then finding out your muscle-fiber type makes sense. It will save you pouring a great deal of time and effort into fruitless pursuits. But if you're running for yourself —for your body, your head, your well-being and sense of self-worth—then fiber type has no more to do with anything than whether you've got brown eyes or blue ones.

That's the way with cocktail-party facts. They're fun, but the proper response always is, So what?

THE ELIXIR OF EXCELLENCE

The urge to race overwhelmed me in middle age, and I competed hard for about five years, chasing (and not catching) a national title. I thought I was just going racing, but what I was really doing was learning how training works. To my surprise, the training part, which was supposed to be so boring, turned out to be a lot more interesting than the racing. Competition was great fun, but it was sheer excitement, rushing past almost too fast to think about it. Training was something I could plan, adjust, experiment with. Training is the part you can be creative with, and creativity is the best antidote I know for boredom.

More important, I never would have understood the nuts and bolts of training—even in the strictest academic sense, as in the progressive loading of the organism—if I hadn't gone racing. Until I began working within competition's framework, enlisting its powers of focus, training wouldn't come together for me. I couldn't conceive of the patience required; I didn't understand how regular and consistent the effort would have to be to nail down the gain. One beautiful thing about competition is its power to codify, clarify, objectify your physical effort. Before I went racing, I couldn't get a grip. I didn't have the mental stamina.

I'm still not sure how I feel about the competitive urge, but racing taught me how deep is the human well from which it springs. Maybe "human" isn't the right word; you see fierce competitiveness in puppies at play, and in most other developmental processes in the animal kingdom. You see it in nature itself; even trees compete with each other for sunlight. It's a kind of elixir of excellence—or at least a powerful goad. When it is not suppressed, as in the truly wild creatures, it produces remarkable athletes. And why not? How hard would you train for that next 10K if you knew that the losers would be eaten?

RECORDS

Some of the "world records" established for the Guinness book seem a little silly—what is the distance record for catching an olive in an open mouth?—but the real ones, in the classic events, represent an amazing glimpse of history. Consider one hundred meters. We've been sprinting that distance for goodness knows how many years. An inconceivable number of people have made a timed run at it. But the record has come down—inched down, millimetered down—very slowly. Wherever the record rests at any given moment, it represents a kind of evolutionary chart, the winnowing of all those attempts over all those years into one single, eloquent number.

WATERING UP, WATERING DOWN

It is dinned into us at running clinics and workshops, by race organizers and medical staffs: drink more water. We see elite athletes get into trouble for lack of it, learn of life-threatening incidents, but we still don't do it. We know we should, but as we hurry past the water tables, it's just too much lost time, too much trouble. When we try we choke for air, stumble, lose our rhythm. Besides, late in the race the discomfort of thirst is more manageable than the other discomforts we're feeling.

The last excuse is the dangerous one, of course; if you're thirsty you're already in trouble, and it is trouble that you can't get out of, that can only worsen, if you continue to exert yourself. To compound the danger, dehydration very quickly makes you stupid. Just when you really need your wits to extract yourself from this physiological mess you've gotten yourself into, you start losing IQ points. It can't be said too often: learn to drink more water.

Envision the process. The body core must be protected from excess heat, and working muscles generate a great deal of heat. Blood circulation, which brings energy supplies to those muscles, also helps carry the heat away. When circulation becomes insufficient, we sweat in order to use surface evaporation for more cooling. When sweating becomes insufficient, we have heat stroke, which quickly becomes fatal.

More commonly we suffer from heat exhaustion. That happens when sweating, plus the substantial amount of liquid blown off in respiration, deplenishes the body's fluid balance. Some of the liquid loss comes out of the blood. If we don't replenish that balance, reduced volume makes the blood thicker, more viscous, harder to pump. To maintain sufficient blood pressure to the vital organs, superficial circulation—to the large muscles, the ones you run with—shuts down. Your athletic effort rapidly comes to a halt. Blood to your higher brain centers is also shut down, which means your judgment about continuing—and about getting out of trouble —also rapidly runs out on you.

Elite athletes get elite treatment: there's always plenty of water for the front-runners, and they're not out there that long anyway. It's us midpackers and back markers who really have to plan our liquid intake. We don't have the tremendous training, the tremendous reserves, of the superstars. We don't zip through marathons in two hours plus and then dive for the shade. And by the time we reach the aid stations all that good volunteer labor has started to lose interest in the whole affair—or run out of supplies.

Heat exhaustion is a form of shock; the symptoms are irritability, dizziness, nausea, headache, and clammy skin. If you recognize any of these symptoms in yourself, get into the shade, lie down, put your feet up, wet down your skin (with ice water if you have it), and drink water slowly.

If you notice these symptoms in another runner, urge the same treatment. Once you're in trouble you can't accurately judge your own state, and you can't expect someone else to do any better. Don't be bashful: we've got to look out for each other.

THE EASIEST WAY

Some of us find that doing a difficult thing the easiest way possible is the most intense physical fun we can have, with the possible exception of sex.

Peculiarly, much of athletic training requires doing hard things the hardest way possible, in order to achieve maximum improvement. It is only when you are competing that you want to find the easiest way. In fact the task of training is to expend yourself as thoroughly as possible in order to cash in on the miracle of adaptation: recovery to a level of fitness superior to the starting point. This can get boring when you don't have the intriguing problem of finding ways to spare yourself. Undertaking a task for no other purpose than to exhaust yourself is not the most physical fun you can have. Perhaps that's why most people find racing more enjoyable than training.

WHERE THE WALLS ARE

There's a benefit to be gained from racing that is not often mentioned: it gives you an easy familiarity with your own capacities, also known as limits. You develop the ability to discern, subjectively, not only the level of effort at which improvement starts but also the level at which it begins to turn sour: a feel for that subtle switchover point from gain to loss. Racing, and the training for it, gives you a comfortable sense of the size of the room within which your efforts are reasonable and effective. It shows you where the walls are.

PUMPS

Cooling down from a run on a ninety-degree day, with humidity to match, I find myself thinking about pumps. The ambient air feels a little squishy, somewhat liquefied; this morning the world seems a particularly fluid place.

A spell of inactivity can have the same effect. If I sit around too long, I begin to get the sense I might drown in my own bilge. Time to man the pumps—in this case the leg muscles, so fundamentally contributory to venous return, so ingeniously designed to aid in the freshening of the blood. Particularly that blood that has been sloshing around in my lower body, gathering wastes but lacking the drive to carry them off for disposal.

In a sense we are nothing but a collection of pumps anyway—a pair of big ones, bellows, for moving gases, and then an endless succession of intricately interlinked hydraulic systems. Sure, there's some wiring for control purposes, and a framework to hang it all on. The work, though, is done by tubes and pumps, shuffling fluids from place to place. (The mind, said the mythologist Joseph Campbell, is a secondary organ.) This metaphor does not extend to the muscle itself, whose contraction is more mechanical than hydraulic. But you have to pump blood to the muscles to start them contracting, to keep them at it, and to give them a chance to relax and contract again. We pump ourselves into motion, pump ourselves along, pump our way to health. (There's a reproductive function that is trying to introduce itself into this metaphor along about here, but I'll leave that to your imagination.)

Anyway, motion not only distinguishes us from plant matter, it is the business that keeps us alive. The more motion you get, the better off you're going to be—even if the motion is only of your bodily fluids. The more alive you'll be, anyway. This is a prescription for health that might not pass the surgeon general's office or the AMA, but I find it a powerful tool for getting myself up and out and moving again.

THE ANNALS OF SPAGHETTI,
PART I

A nutritionist at your elbow, complete with an accurate scale, can't tell within three hundred calories what you're consuming per day, and that large an error can add thirty pounds in a year. Dieting is crazy.

Exercise isn't. By burning off fat you become leaner. The leaner you are, the more calories you burn just sitting still, since lean mass has a higher metabolic rate than fat. Exercise is a more powerful kick to the wheel of life than its mere fuel cost can possibly explain. Runners are fond of explaining this, usually around a mouthful of spaghetti.

ENERGY BUDGETS

In nature the energy budget is primal law, the absolute bottom line. Energy supply, energy availability, governs every single living thing. Humans are no different, once you take away our civilized veneer of overprotection. Put us in a truly elemental situation—as on mountaineering or exploratory expeditions, or even in ultra-distance running—and the energy budget becomes the driving force in our lives, too. It immediately replaces sex, money, power, religion, politics, or any of those other motivations we've developed to keep our metaphorical motors running. The calculations that govern success or failure for that level of effort have precisely to do with calories in and calories out. It's the metabolic equivalent of cash flow—and when you're out there on the edge, bankruptcy doesn't mean embarrassment and inconvenience, it means death.

WHEN FATIGUE HELPS

To a certain extent each of us runs the way we're built to run, and changes to stride in search of efficiency will necessarily be subtle. We should work to reduce the amount of up-and-down motion, to keep our flailing arms, head, and neck under control, to get our feet back down smoothly onto the road. Strangely, the best lessons usually come when we're most tired: fatigue can teach us where effort is being misplaced.

THE INCLINOMETER

The first mile of my favorite run winds gradually uphill. There are a few flat spots along the way, but the general trend is upward. By the time I get to one particular flat—an abandoned sawmill site, now all grown up again and surrounded by shady maples—I've usually pulled my shirt off, or, in other seasons, made some other adjustment to my clothing. The absolute dependability of the furnace of the body—and the absolute dependability of an uphill stretch to crank up that furnace—never fails to impress me.

There's a gadget called an inclinometer that tells how many degrees the axis of a ship or an airplane is inclined in relation to the horizontal. I hereby propose body heat as the runner's inclinometer. I haven't a clue how you'd calibrate it—some scientist with a treadmill could probably solve that quickly enough—but how hot you get tells you pretty clearly how much of a hill you've been climbing. And running downhill will cool you off as dependably as it lets you get your breath back. You simply stop burning so much fuel.

Hills only exacerbate the problem, of course.

We runners don't always give it much conscious thought, but one of the largest management challenges in our sport is to retain body heat when we need it and to get rid of it when we don't. If you run year-round in a temperate climate, it's as if you're always somewhere between hypothermia and heat injury. Either extreme means serious trouble. In fact, if you haven't learned how to retain and disperse heat as needed, you're asking for an ambulance ride.

Ambulances are sometimes available at races and organized runs, but if you get into trouble when you're out there on your own, you may be depending on someone to find your unconscious body.

THE GLORIES OF MUSCLE

A curious thing about muscle is that although it has the power to control the incredibly smooth and graceful movements of dance, of such sports as diving and figure skating, it is in fact digital: it is on or off. If a muscle fiber is stimulated sufficiently to contract, it does so all the way; no half-measures. This is the all-or-none law of physiology.

The law applies, however, only to individual fibers, not to the muscle as a unit. Smoothness of movement—the product of exquisite choices in gradation of force or length of contraction—is possible because muscle fibers are bound up into units, and not all the fibers in the muscle unit are fired at the same time.

We can hardly be runners without pondering the curiosities of muscle. After all, it's the enabler, the effector, the suit of power that allows us to get out there on the road. It is the part of us most easily accessible to training, not to mention the part that must be trained to make running enjoyable. It adapts to running as if that's what it was designed for—and as a matter of fact, anthropologists suspect that this is precisely the case.

In fact we must train muscle, or at least keep using it, to maintain its viability. Clip the nerve that fires it and it loses its tone—the steady, low-level tension that keeps it cocked and ready for action—and begins to die. This is known as the atrophy of denervation. Immobilize the muscle—put it in a cast—and it will also atrophy, this time from the atrophy of disuse. Denervation is irreversible, however; disuse is not. The muscle can recover from disuse if you will only put it to work. And there you have the first principle of exercise physiology spelled out in block letters: WORK IS REQUIRED TO KEEP THE MUSCLE ALIVE.

I once asked Tom McMahon, the biomechanist who designed a series of tuned running tracks in the 1980s, why muscle so fascinated scientists like himself. Oh, muscle is terribly important, he told me. "We're only alive because our hearts pump blood and our diaphragms pump air and we have the ability to move," he said. "That's all muscle. Maybe you prefer to say we're alive because our brain works, but I really think the brain was designed to coordinate the activities of the muscle."

IN PRAISE OF SORENESS

Stick to running, says the more sensible part of my brain; those other activities always make you sore. It's true enough. To change the mode of exercise is to discover a startling assortment of unused muscles. And soreness can be terribly depressing, with its implication of loss of function, otherwise known as aging.

There's an argument in favor of soreness,

however. We exercise to stay alive—to be more alive, to get more use out of ourselves—and in that sense, minor-grade muscular soreness is only an indication, an index, of the amount of life that's been taking place in those structures. Delayed-onset soreness is an old friend, telling us not only that we've spent a little interesting effort but that the tissues we spent it with are now busier places. There's a little more of the business of life going on in them.

That's "life" in the objective, scientific sense: more exchanges going on, more materials being processed, more actions being taken. The pain that may result is the subjective part. Soreness, you might say, is the subjective reading on how much objective work you've done. How lively you've been. Personally, I can live with a reminder of that now and then.

SINEW

Running is use; running without sufficient recovery time is overuse, and overuse injuries are the plague of the physically active. When overuse injuries occur, they strike connective tissue first. Connective tissue is everything in you that isn't muscle, fluid, or nerve. (Even bone is connective tissue; overuse injuries to it are called stress fractures.) But the connective tissue that takes the worst beating is tendon: what we used to call sinew.

Unfortunately for runners, the foot, the heel, and the knee are most vulnerable to tendinitis. (Achilles tendinitis is the single most common athletic injury.) The foot is a complicated bag of bones, capable of movement in almost as many planes as the shoulder. If any of those movements are misaligned, extra stress is put on the Achilles, the tendons of the foot, and the knee. That means that if your Achilles is strong enough to stand the load, the stresses of misalignment will be passed along to some other connective tissue. Plantar fasciitis is one result; so are heel spurs and runner's knee. But the Achilles gets most of the grief.

Hence the warnings about running in worn-out shoes. Any misalignment, from bad equipment, bad technique, or bad feet, will result in some kind of overload. Good sound shoes are just the most sensible—and the least-expensive—starting point. They'll help you take care of your sinews. Do that and keep moving, and the rest of you will take care of itself.

FINISHING

Cool-down considerations aside, there's a natural tendency to finish off a run with a burst of speed. You've expended all this effort, you're tired, but it seems only fitting somehow to pick up the pace at the end. Might as well go ahead and empty out the vessel. Finishing strong is dependably satisfying, even if all it says is that you didn't push hard enough along the way.

Consider it the macro-version of a basic athletic principle, the micro-version of which improves and informs every athletic move. In downhill skiing, for instance, great emphasis is placed on finishing one turn in order to get the next one started right. When I heard that, I didn't understand. You have to stop turning one way if you're going to start turning the other, don't you? How could you do otherwise? I flailed and flummoxed my way through a lot of awkward moments before the significance of the advice sank in. A properly completed turn, carried to its logical physical conclusion, ends in an edge-set that gives you a stable platform from which to start the next turn. "Finished" means your weight is in the right place—your body and skis prepared—for whatever comes next. Without that preparation you're in trouble.

It's the same in any sport. Finishing moves is hard to learn because when a sport is new, the moves come too fast, keeping you rushed, confused. When you aren't sure you have time to get the next move started, you know you don't have time to fool around finishing one that's virtually over with. It's only when the moves begin to become linked, serialized, automatic, that you can see the lovely contradiction: taking the time to finish one move properly always gives you more time for the next.

This investment in time—and investment is precisely what it is—is the very thing that makes finishing well so difficult. In the macro-version—near the end of a 10K, say, or any other endurance event—it means spending time in a rapidly intensifying discomfort zone. Spending time there, and dealing with the discomfort that results, can be difficult, but it is also fascinating. It is the essential province of the distance runner, the specific lure around which endurance sports are built.

It is the part that instruction manuals can't tell you anything about. You have to learn for yourself, subjectively, what it feels like to reach down and turn the screws a little tighter. You feel the rise of the discomfort levels, and, investigating their content, learn to your surprise that they need not stop you. You can live with them. And then you turn the screw one turn tighter, searching for the edge. Finishing well is a visit to Edge City, every time.

It has been said that heroism is endurance for one moment longer. Heroism for itself can be a dubious goal, but a visit to Edge City seldom is. Not a nice place (and you certainly would not want to live there), but it's where you find out who it is that's doing the finishing.

WHEN SILENCE IS DANGEROUS

Do not ignore your cholesterol count. Just because you run and therefore feel so good, because you know that as long as you keep up the daily run you can do whatever you want, you think you can indulge yourself to your heart's content. Heart's content, as it turns out, is a little different from belly's content. Be advised: listening to your body is fine as far as it goes, but your heart has a way of remaining silent until the damage is done.

MOLECULAR THEORY

Kelp and algae and bee pollen and all the rest of the fad foods may very well be different, even highly unusual, mixtures of the molecules that are found in, oh, corn, or beef, or spinach, or any of the rest of the mundane diet of ordinary folk. But it is as molecules, and only as molecules, that the cells are able to make use of those nutrients, and several million years of evolution have made those cells pretty well able to sort out the mix for themselves.

The mitochondria want carbohydrates (among other things); the idea that they're not going to get the goody out of those carbohydrates, or that they're going to be poisoned by them, if they come in the form of white sugar, for example, is not persuasive.

LIKE THE WIND

The Chiricahua Apache, who fought the final Indian wars on American soil in the last decades of the nineteenth century, were eventually rounded up and sent to concentration camps in

Florida and Alabama. A quarter of their number died of disease in the first three years of their imprisonment; after five more debilitating years in the Deep South they were removed to Fort Sill in Oklahoma.

When they got to Fort Sill they learned that mesquite trees, the beans of which had furnished a staple of their homeland diet, and which they hadn't tasted in eight years, were growing forty-five miles away. They asked for and were given permission to harvest the beans. A group of them left on foot and, walking and jogging the ninety-mile round trip, returned forty-eight hours later, carrying three hundred bushels of the beans.

In their warlike days the Apache preferred horseback, but war parties would sometimes go on foot to maintain the element of surprise, routinely covering forty to forty-five miles a day. When their horses had been lost to pursuing cavalry, they would somehow maintain the same pace, day after day, carrying their own supplies or living off the land—and taking their women and children with them. Geronimo once led a band of fugitives, including women and children and with virtually no food, for sixty nonstop miles, baffling their mounted pursuers.

During the period when they were still confined to reservations in Arizona, one of their white overseers was surprised when a sixty-year-old Apache woman approached him with a wild turkey in her arms, as a gift. She'd run it down on foot.

These anecdotes come from *Once They Moved Like the Wind,* by David Roberts. In it Roberts documents the training of Chiricahua youths, not only in the arts of hunting and warfare but specifically in physical fitness. "A boy's fitness training began in earnest at age eight," Roberts says. "He would be forced to get up before dawn to run to the top of a mountain and back before sunrise. He might run as far as four miles with a mouthful of water he was not allowed to swallow, or with his mouth full of pebbles. As a kind of graduation exam, a boy undertook a two-day cross-country run without food or sleep."

A little more rigorous than my last preparation for a 10K, I admit, but then I've never had the U.S. Cavalry chasing me. Geronimo did—five thousand of them in one campaign, plus three thousand Mexican soldiers and assorted scouts and volunteers, a force totaling, according to Roberts, "nearly nine thousand armed men pursuing eighteen Chiricahua warriors, thirteen women, and six children." They pursued the fugitives for five months, over something like three thousand miles, and captured not a single Apache.

That, folks, is distance running.

A PENNY SAVED

Employers now know that fitness is cheaper than health care. It costs less to provide exercise facilities and time to use them than it does to pay for the absenteeism and hospital bills that accompany the nonexercising life.

If the employees don't stick with the program, though, the boss ends up paying for both.

TONE

Skilled movement is possible only if the muscle can read its own state of tension: it must be informed, in contact with itself. The contact is maintained, the muscle kept at the ready—cocked, in effect—by muscle tone, a low level of contraction maintained by signals from a neural loop called the gamma system. Keep the signal turned on and tone takes up the muscle's slack, keeping it purring away at idle, ready to respond without lurching.

Good muscle tone works as a buffer against the shock of sudden action, absorbing forces that can, over time, prove harmful to the less elastic tissue of tendons and ligaments. But it is more than a shock absorber: it is part of our very liveliness, the simple underlying tautness that keeps us quick and responsive to the world.

Of course maintaining muscle tone requires nothing more than that we continue to move. But runners have always suspected something like that, haven't we?

MUSCLE "PULLS"

Most athletic injuries don't happen to muscle but to connective tissue. Sprains, strains, stress fractures, fasciitis, tendinitis—all are injuries to connective tissue. Even the so-called muscle "tear" or "pull" is more a rupture of the connective tissue that holds the muscle than it is of the muscle itself.

THE BREAK-OVER POINT

In any exercise program there comes a break-over point, before which to continue is painful, after which to continue is exhilarating. When that happens a lot of other things —not just running—somehow get a little easier. Actually, it's the point at which you realize that a new platform of energy has been run under your life. Once you reach it you're much less likely to drop out: you remember too well the foggy veil that would descend again if you did.

There ought to be a way to study that break-over point. I haven't seen it specifically identified, but some clever scientist ought to be able to pinpoint and describe the actual physiology for it.

THE APPLICATION OF PAIN

My route is uphill on a hot, sticky day, so I start out slowly, waiting for my body to catch up with the hill. I'm hoping, in other words, to minimize that testy little period of distress that always occurs before respiration, circulation, body temperature, and all those other variables get balanced out.

Slow running leads to long thoughts. Athletic events that have to do with speed or stamina require the negotiation of periods of distress. When coaches talk about "character," they're usually referring to the amount of equanimity one brings to these periods.

The tough thing about competition, though, is that you have to keep the pain from lessening. To achieve your maximum you must keep applying pain. This is an aspect of athletic performance that I don't like to think about too much. It smacks of a kind of totalitarian over-commitment. The truth is, however, that if you want to be an athlete, if you want to perform better, this is the territory in which you must operate. These are the variables from which you fashion higher performance.

As a swimmer I competed in races that lasted anywhere from twenty-five seconds (50 meters) to twenty minutes (1500 meters). Thinking back, I started to say there were distinct waves of distress that occurred periodically throughout the race, whatever its length. But that only happened when I was a newcomer and didn't know the pace. Once you know the pace for a given event, you just hit it and hold it—and then try to squeeze a little more out of it. The pain comes once—early—and, basically, stays. You try to hold it steady. You know that if it gets too bad you'll tie up and be out of the race, and if it gets too easy you'll be left behind. Finally I learned that, but I never particularly liked it. Maybe that's why I'm not racing anymore.

Some athletes deal with pain by considering that they're applying it not to themselves but to their competitors. I'm not sure I like this idea either. If you believe that, then you have to believe that the pain you feel is being applied by your competitors. I don't want to put the controls of the pain machine in someone else's hands.

Racing finally taught me that finding that cusp—the point where the pain is continuous but bearable, where it's just short of stopping you—is the object of the game. But when I learned that I also learned that finding it and riding it—keeping the pressure on, discovering that you can not only continue but can squeeze it a little tighter—is the best thing that happens in competition. I don't know about you, but I found that to be a bigger thrill than winning.

OBSESSION—AND OTHER PERFUMES

Every day some new thing seems to get labeled "addictive." We're busily finding more and more things—behaviors as well as substances—that people find they prefer not to do without. Every now and then running is included in that category.

It is fairly clear that the body's cells and their needs can actually be changed by nothing more than long-term, gradually accumulating exposure to an agent of change. Running is an agent of change. So maybe we're addicted to it. So what? So we're going to be miserable if we have to stop. Most of us were miserable before we started—and won't be miserable, at least in that same way, until we do have to stop.

Is this obsessive behavior? Goodness, I hope so. I figure all I really have the right to ask of life is to be fully engaged by it. If that means going at things a little obsessively, well, maybe that's the price you pay. Haven't those worry-warts ever noticed how happy we obsessives are?

"Sisyphus was basically a happy man."
—Albert Camus

MOODS, PART II

"Muscular movements initiate stimuli in muscle spindles which are essential for optimal functioning of the central nervous system," I once copied down from a long-lost physiology text. There you have an argument for a more physical life. You don't often get it that way from the exercise gurus, but it expresses a truth we all know, if not in our muscles then in our guts. Or our hearts. "There appears to be a relationship between an individual's mood and his muscle condition and posture," the text goes on to say. I've never seen a clearer statement of what might be called the deep reason—one of the deep reasons—for running.

US WEAKLINGS

Runners have a tendency to assume that running provides all the exercise we need—and besides, no one but a professional athlete has time for a truly comprehensive exercise program. This is a sound philosophy if all you ever do is run. If you do anything else, particularly if you anticipate doing something else that has a demanding physical component to it, it's a good idea to consider strength training. If all you ever do is run, you are—believe it or not—an absolute tower of weak muscles.

MOANS AND GROANS

Circumstances recently kept me from my stretching routine for five days. On the sixth, walking through the kitchen, some impulse made me grab the refrigerator door and sag sideways away from it, stretching the muscles between my offside ribs. The sensation sent me into a virtual coma of pleasure, writhing and moaning, getting at tissues that hadn't had any real relief in days. I couldn't believe the cramped and tightened state I was in; I couldn't get over the pleasure available from finally stretching out to full length again.

I stretch by habit. For the past twenty years or so I've done it virtually every day. I've done it in hotels and other people's living rooms, in airport corridors, on swimming pool decks and in health clubs, alongside jogging paths, once even in an ashram. I've done it nude and in street clothes, by myself and in groups, before, during, and after runs. It took a five-day moratorium to show me how strong the addiction is.

Trying to sell the pleasures of stretching to nonbelievers, I have learned, is a pointless pursuit. The world is divided into stretchers and nonstretchers—genetically determined, perhaps—and nobody switches sides. Those of us who stretch seem to have a pleasure center accessible by no other route; firing its nerve endings becomes a necessity for sustaining mobility, if not life itself. Those who stretch know that those who don't have no idea what they're missing.

Discovering—rediscovering—the ecstasies available from hanging off the refrigerator sent me staggering around the kitchen, grabbing this support or that, tugging and hauling at my reawakened connective tissue. The best result came from placing my hands on the kitchen counter—that perfect stretching barre—and bending at the waist. Arms, legs, and back straight, making an inverted L, I could stretch rib cage, hamstrings, and shoulder sockets all at the same time. I became lost in the sheer sensual pleasure of pulling constricted tissue back out to length. Considering the groans and exultations wrenched unbidden from my mouth, I'm surprised my wife didn't come running; the cats certainly scattered. The kitchen lights even seemed to dim; what was happening used to be called a swoon, produced by nothing more than the stretch receptors in my joints—signaling relief, liberation, freedom.

My theory of stretching—so far impervious to scientific proof—is fairly simple: just as muscle is maintained by contraction, connective tissue is maintained by tension. By pulling on the stuff. It is so much more than tendon and ligament. It is the sheathing that organizes muscles into coherent units, the webbing that holds the physiology together, the organizing principle of the body. To stay healthy, it must be used. Stretching is the most manageable way of using it. That the act of stretching happens to feel so good is pure bonus. I'm addicted, all right—and it's one monkey I want never to get off my back.

MORE BUDGETING

"Racing is like building a house. The first ninety percent of the race takes ninety percent of your resources. The remaining ten percent of the race takes another ninety percent of your resources."   —Ron Cross

STUPIDITIES

That old argument over whether or not athletes are smart is almost always a duel of wits between unarmed persons. Note the plural: neither side is likely to have sufficient ammunition, or information. If they did, the argument would quickly evaporate. The jocks-are-stupid point of view hasn't a clue to the complexity of the problem-solving that athletes must bring to bear on their particular tasks; the jocks-are-smart side can't conceive of the level of abstraction, not to mention denial, at work among people who have no interest in the physical side of things.

At the risk of further revealing my own bias, I must admit I use the word "physical" more in the sense of physics than in the sense of bodily effort. The beauty part of athletic endeavor for me is not in the grunting expenditure of energy, but in the interplay of that effort with the phenomenal world, where the hard laws of time and space, of energy and matter, are all that count. Athletics is about operating that world, about getting the most out of it—and getting the most out of yourself as well, as a participating member of it. Running or any other athletic endeavor can be as brainy an undertaking as you care to make it.

That doesn't mean, however, that an utter dolt can't enjoy sports as exuberantly as the brainiest person who ever lived. I can testify to this from personal experience.

HEART

For a life with more life in it—more capacity —you train the heart; everything else follows. The details can be intricate, but the principle is not exactly rocket science. To do more you have to burn more fuel; to burn more fuel you need more oxygen; to get more oxygen to the furnaces where fuel is burned you must move more blood; to move more blood your heart has to do more work. You make the heart able to do more work by working it. A well-trained heart pumps more blood with each stroke, accomplishing more work with less energy expenditure. By beating more slowly it gets a chance to rest. The more it rests, the stronger it gets.

Thus working the heart unleashes a chain of improvement throughout the entire cardiovascular system—lungs, arterial walls, capillaries, oxygen-transport system, energy-production enzymes and regulatory hormones, all the little bits and pieces that make the processes of air-breathing and blood-using more efficient. And thence, simply because more is happening throughout yourself, to all the other systems you've got.

Lucky us. My wife suggests I hang a small sign on my typewriter that says, MOVE, STUPID.

GIMME A BREAK

Repetition and routine make the neural circuits tired, whatever the nature of the task. The only way to get a fresh start is to use different circuits for a while. Shooting the breeze around the water cooler may drive bosses crazy but it shouldn't: it's exactly enough break to resharpen manual dexterity or wits or vision or whatever it is that goes stale when one sticks too long to a task. To say nothing about maintaining proper hydration, which is more of a factor in efficiency, in consistent performance, than most employers dream. Unless they're marathoners.

Employers might be astonished at what happened to productivity if workers could find a congenial way to take a little oxygen break from time to time. It's something that runners already know.

BELLIES

Science is looking into bellies. Men tend to put away extra fat in their paunches, women gain in buttocks and thighs. The theory is that thunder-thighs store energy for pregnancy and breast-feeding, paunches for long hunts—and periodic famines. Thigh and buttock fat is harder to get rid of because it's laid up for the long, slow haul; belly fat is the kind of energy store that a marathoner needs. This doesn't mean you'll improve in the marathon if you lug around a heavy gut, though. All else being equal, the competitor who weighs the least will finish first. It does mean that running will burn off belly fat before it will burn off thigh and buttock fat.

But don't celebrate yet, guys: people with paunches are at higher cardiovascular risk than people who carry their fat elsewhere. Science isn't sure why, but fat stored in the gut is particularly responsive to stress hormones. These fight-or-flight chemicals release fuel—in the form of fatty acids, derived from fat stores—directly to the bloodstream, where it can lead eventually to high blood pressure, diabetes, and heart problems. There is small comfort in the fact that you can reduce this fat by running: you're asking for trouble if you don't.

BORED HORSES

Interval work is now being used to train trotting horses, and racing speeds in that sport have risen. Equine athletic physiologists can't pinpoint physical changes from that training, however, that would explain the improvement. Some trainers think intervals work on the head, rather than the body: the horse doesn't get so bored, and will therefore put in more quality work.

WILLPOWER—AND GLYCOGEN

The reporter was working on one of those human-interest stories about masters athletes, the older the better. Isn't it backbone, he asked, that gives some of these ancient competitors an edge? When the chips are down, don't their age and experience give them more pure willpower?

More likely it's glycogen, I said, amazed at the question. My amazement was compounded with nostalgia: the question comes right out of what might be called Boys' Lit. You know, those books you read in junior high school, in which our hero finally triumphs over the hated cross-town rivals? Thanks, usually, to a providential dollop of second wind?

Boys' Lit breaks a lot of hearts. I know, it bruised mine once, when I was sixteen and went out too fast in the swimming equivalent of the 800-meter run. I ran out of gas, of course, and, without the first glimmer of how athletic physiology actually works, I blamed my lack of willpower. Boys' Lit had taught me that if I'd really wanted it badly enough I'd have found the guts to hold the pace. Boys' Lit never mentioned lactic acid.

Second wind is a wonderfully Calvinist notion. Stick to your task, be pure of heart, and you will be rewarded by a kind of divine cancellation of the laws of physiology. The curious thing is that something like second wind does happen, but only nonathletes notice it. Folks who seldom experiment with their own physical limits may experience a physiological lift the first few times they do. Start slowly enough, give the systems a chance to balance out, and eventually you may notice a mildly euphoric blast of energy, allowing you to continue when you thought you could not. The worse shape you're in, the earlier it kicks in (and, unfortunately, the earlier it runs out again).

Conversely, the better shape you're in, the less likely you are even to notice this miraculous phenomenon. All it is is the small transaction, every time you go for a run, that lets you know you're truly warmed up. There may be other transactions—third winds, fourth winds, an infinity of winds—that buoy the athlete's spirits and allow late bursts of heightened effort, but no one has succeeded in measuring one on a treadmill. The boost is psychological rather than physiological, which makes it a lot harder to train for.

Check the back markers in a marathon and you'll see a lot of folks dragging grimly along, waiting for one more "wind" to come along. This may be where the willpower comes in, but it doesn't have much to do with explaining why some athletes perform better than others. When you tie up, you tie up. Willpower may get you to the finish line, which is a victory in itself, but the people you beat are the ones who have less glycogen available than you do, not less character.

No point in trying to explain this to the reporter. I told him that if successful older athletes have an edge in willpower, it is applied during training, not in the race. Training takes place at the level of the cell. The character has to be applied before the performance.

I haven't gone back to the Young Adult section to see if Boys' Lit—or Girls' Lit, for that matter—has discovered lactic acid, but it might be an interesting new development. You want to beat the Hated Crosstown Rival? Try interval-training, kiddo. That's what those wonderful old athletes do.

$N = 1$

The symbol n is the number in the sample. Science wants a large n, in order to make its predictions more statistically valid. When you want to find out what works for your individual self, however, you have to venture beyond probabilities.

Nobody else's training program can possibly be the best for you; to achieve that you just have to keep experimenting. On yourself. When we run we are doing science with an *n* of one. When it comes to your own running—your own life—it's the only *n* that counts.

HEALING

Strangely enough, rehabilitation of injury and athletic training are really two sides of the same coin. Some cynics regard training, in the sense of deliberately applied stress, as a kind of controlled damage, but I think that's far too pessimistic. Instead, we might very well think of regular, consistent, programmatic athletic training—one favorite form of which is distance running—as healing after you've already healed. It is healing of injuries you may not know you have: the injuries of modern, sedentary, high-pressure life.

More important, training is a kind of healing of injuries you haven't suffered yet. Look at it this way: running is healing ahead of time, before the fact.

WALLET PROTECTION, PART II

Runners run, as armies march, on their stomachs. In fact we fill our stomachs in order to run, since all muscular energy comes from the conversion of food into fuel. Some of us turn this right around and run in order to go on filling our stomachs. To us, "healthy" eating is "Gimme another slice of that pizza, will you, and make it a real healthy one."

It would be nice if there were some real intelligence to offer here on the subject of nutrition, but frankly I've never run across any. Science knows an enormous amount about metabolism —the use to which the gut puts all that food we stuff into it—but when it comes to what stuff that ought to be, you get a mixture of contradiction and mumbo jumbo. All we really know is that we should cut down on fats and eat as wide a variety of foods as possible, preferably unprocessed. When it comes to specific recommendations, war immediately breaks out between the food police and the various dairy, citrus, grain, meat, and other lobbies. When someone starts advising you on what to eat, it's a good idea to put your hand over your wallet, if not over your mouth.

When you're warming up legs and lungs, it wouldn't hurt to wiggle the spine around a bit while you're at it. The only circulatory system that the spinal fluid has is skeletal movement; you keep the stuff moving almost as a side effect of moving yourself. This is the soup that keeps the disks moist and springy, preventing nerve damage; the serum that keeps all those facets of all those joints between all those vertebrae sufficiently bathed in lubricants to keep you from creaking to a halt; the liquor that delivers the spine's own special nutrients and hauls off its peculiar wastes. It can always use a little help.

NOW

Most of us spend our working hours making judgments about the future—will this work pass muster, what work must I do next, how can I provide for a better life. It's that requirement for a future orientation, I think, that makes running such a relief. It is physical, it is real, and it happens right now, when you do it. You have no choice: you have to run in the present tense.

STALE

When you go stale at your work, the best thing you can possibly do is go for a run. Nothing else so effectively clears the head.

The wonderful thing is how the break gets finished before the run does. Work requires that you strain at concentration, trying to keep your mind focused on the task at hand. That's the tiring part. When you decide to stop and go for a run, you let all that go, forget about it, direct your attention to completely different matters.

But running doesn't take that much attention, so before long you quit focusing on that, too. Before you know it, your mind is thinking about any darned thing it wants to, and you are merely plodding along behind, more or less amused to see what turns up. Invariably it works its way back around to the problem at hand— the work you're taking a break from—and starts going at it from some fresh new direction.

IV

FALL

I ran into a hunter the other day. Ran by him, that is, and wished I hadn't. Not that there was any confrontation; I just came across a man with a gun, walking along what I'd come to think of as my own personal running trail in the woods. We exchanged nothing more than a glance, but the mood was spoiled. That the woods contain people carrying arms is not the sort of thing I like to contemplate while running there. It's not conducive to free-and-easy mileage. Come to think of it, I probably didn't do much for his mood, either—damned runners, galloping around, scaring off the game.

Few runners, I suspect, are also hunters, which is strange, in a way. Surely long-distance running is a development right out of our hunter-gatherer heritage—although not, perhaps, the gatherer part. You don't have to stay on the trail of an apple for hours at a time. Wheat isn't going to run away from you. But following the herd—in order to run down and pick off its weaker members, which is nature's own favorite scheme for ensuring the fitness of both hunter and quarry species—would seem to call for distance running. Or for running in general: sprinting, too, would be required for running the prey to earth.

The closest we can come to understanding man's own aboriginal hunting techniques, according to Barry Lopez, is to watch wolves hunt. Wolves are capable of tremendous feats of running. A pack will cover thirty to forty miles a day, every day, delivering food to a female confined to the den. An Eskimo on a snowmobile has documented chasing a wolf for twenty kilometers, at speeds between twenty-five and fifty kilometers per hour: consecutive 10Ks, in other words, in under twenty minutes each. On snow.

There is in human nature an implied, or perhaps imagined, progression from competition to aggression to violence. It's not an implication I'm fond of. If we take the biological view, as in wolves and caribou, then hunting isn't so much violence as it is an orderly transaction, carried out between naturally acting species (although it probably doesn't seem that way to the caribou). Today's hunters make the argument that there's something noble in preserving this transaction. I'm not fond of that argument, either. In other areas we've done our best to remove killing from our daily lives. Whether or not such removal is a good thing is moot. Hunting reinserts killing into our experience.

I think it's the killing itself that would drive runners away from hunting. I wouldn't try to make the argument that runners are necessarily less violent than the rest of the population. Runners commit as much immoral silliness as anyone. But in the end, running is an ethic, an act with a moral foundation. Those of us who do it are closet moralists, haranguing the world by example—which may be why we run into hostility from passing motorists.

For the hunter-gatherer, perhaps, running was just a tool; for us, running is about something. What it is about is life: the improvement and the celebration thereof. Running is about defeating death, not inflicting it. I'd be happier if we left the hunting to wolves. Strange, but the thought that wolves might be in the woods isn't half as interruptive of my running pleasure as the one about people with guns.

ON TAKING A LITTLE OFF

If you are inclined to run at all, you're inclined to push yourself. That's simply how it works.

Once you make it past the first few months of running—or for some people the first few weeks—you begin to experience the rewards of increase and improvement. As soon as you start feeling that particular surge, you automatically begin to apply all the pressure on yourself you need. What you may need to pay attention to is taking a little off.

There are personal trainers and coaches who still feel they have to push people—and they may be right, for the kind of clientele that needs their services. It's instructive to compare the personal-trainer approach, aimed at non-athletes, to the way the canny old coach works to get the most out of experienced athletes. Keep it going, says the personal trainer: suck it up, give me three more reps, harder, drive through it, more, more, more. Stay within yourself, says the coach: don't press, take your time, get it right. Take a little off.

We are habitual runners, however: autonomous runners, who have discovered in ourselves the mechanisms for self-starting and self-direction. For us persuasion is no longer necessary. What may be necessary is the opposite: encouragement to cool it. A balanced, harmonious, nonaggressive program is guaranteed to be more satisfactory, over a longer period of time, than the more bullheaded approach. Rest is the most important part of any training program. The work sets up the rest. In athletics as well as architecture, less is sometimes more.

Taking a little off means recognizing that going all out eventually means not going at all. If you go all out all the time, pretty soon it'll be all over, or over at least until your injuries heal. More injuries, more mistakes, more dropouts result from doing too much than too little, from trying too hard than from not trying hard enough. We err more from using too much force than from using too little. More athletic disasters result from starting too early than from starting late, from advancing too fast than too slow. What we need to remember most of all is that we're in this for the long run.

REPETITIVE MOTION

"Repetitive motion disorders," the Labor Department calls them, or "repetitive trauma illnesses." They're increasing faster than any other cause of job-related illness. "Such illnesses result from repeating the same motions with arms and hands throughout the day," says the newspaper, "as occurs on assembly lines and at computer terminals." Carpal tunnel syndrome, for instance: that one happens to bike riders as well as assembly-line operators, although the feds didn't mention that. It results from the pounding the rider's hands and wrists take through the handlebars.

Might as well add feet, legs, shoulders, hips, and backs to the Labor Department's list: stress fractures, tendinitis, plantar or other kinds of fasciitis, runner's knee, tennis elbow, just about every other sports injury you hear of—short of those caused by a single traumatic wrench or blow—can be lumped into this category.

Thus bureaucracy catches up with sports trainers. "Repetitive motion disorder" is bureaucratese for what sports medicine has for decades been calling overuse injury. The only difference, if any, is that repetitive motion disorders happen when you're doing something under the boss's watchful eye and don't have much control over when you can stop and rest, and overuse injuries occur when you're doing something for fun. Or for your health, which is a strange thing to say about something that results in injury. Actually, it's pretty amazing that a job can elicit the same kind of do-it-till-something-gives intensity that a sport can. Says something about the way we have to work these days to keep our heads above water.

VOLUME

If you keep track of your mileage, you'll probably notice an upward bulge in the curve as autumn comes on. This is when runners tend to pile on the work. Days are cooling off, making the miles more pleasant; nature puts on its most vivid display, drawing us outdoors just for the visual treat. Who doesn't want to go for a run on a bright fall morning? Let's rack up some more miles today.

I used to think it was the quality of the air. Serious pollination is over with, the summer's humid exudations having been snapped off sharp by frost. Here and there windfall apples ferment in the grass, adding a whiff of brandy to the stuff we breathe so hard when we run. I figured it was something sensual about this mixture that revved us up, sent us whipping out the door. But it isn't the air that does it, it's the light.

More properly, the angle of the light. The slanting rays of autumn sun signal the onset of winter. In nature there are two strategies for dealing with winter's difficulties: hibernation and migration. If we're not hibernators—and runners obviously are not—then we're migratory, a solution that involves considerable mileage. Migration isn't always Arctic-Circle-to-Central-Mexico; as there are gradations of hibernation, there are also minor-league seasonal migrations too. Bats that live in Indiana migrate to Kentucky, lobsters migrate from shallow water to deep. Pigeons migrate from suburbs to city core, field mice to farmhouse walls. Migration is only the programmed response to the natural impulse to go where food is, where life can be maintained (and extended).

These clear distinctions—hibernators versus migrators—exist only at the extremes anyway. There are families of rats that are highly migratory, and other families of rats of the same species that are highly sedentary. The only innate difference between these two kinds of rats that science can find is the degree of restlessness at puberty. In other words, sex hormones tend to stimulate the migratory urge, too. That's handy: migration is a risky business.

(By some estimates only about ten percent of migrating songbirds survive each year.) The highly sexed, the good breeders, are winnowed out by restlessness to become migrators.

So are runners, surely. I'll pass on the question of whether runners are oversexed, but I'm fairly confident that those of us who become runners had restless adolescences, that we were never that good at sitting still. Autumn—smelling of apples and wood smoke, lit by nature's warning to move on, to go someplace else—doesn't make sitting still any easier.

So what? So in the fall you may find yourself running some particularly delicious extra miles, that's all. Enjoy. Who wouldn't want to go for a run on a bright fall morning?

OLD CATS

The processes of aging are vivid around our house these days. We have a new kitten—in addition to a geriatric cat, a middle-aged dog, and another dog in her prime. Every day we are privileged to watch the young feline discover new physical skills and capabilities, which is inspiring, even thrilling.

Unfortunately, the old cat is losing capacities as fast as the young one is acquiring them, and watching that is not so thrilling. It is, however, a textbook demonstration of the physiology of aging—time-lapse photography, so to speak. Old cats seem to hang on forever, but when their faculties begin to go, it's as if someone pushed the fast-forward button. It is a sad but instructive demonstration of just what it is we're fighting in ourselves.

One reason we have pets is for the enjoyment of being surrounded by such great natural athletes. (Compared to an ordinary house cat, Mikhail Baryshnikov is a stumblebum.) On a recent morning, though, I noticed that the older dog, Molly, was a little tentative, not moving very well. She did a surprisingly bad job of leaping a small brook—and then I, following, did a bad job of it too. It made me realize that I was moving all hunched up, unsure, tense. I wasn't warmed up yet, but that was no excuse. What I was really seeing was that Molly was moving like an old dog, and that I was moving like an old man. Stop it, I told myself. Stop running like a doddering old gaffer. I managed to do it for fifty yards or so, but then I got to thinking about something else, and the first thing I knew my shoulders were up around my ears again. I have a terrible time remembering to stay loose, but then I'm not much of an athlete.

The other day I caught myself rearranging things in the kitchen so I wouldn't have to reach up to the top shelf so often. That's exactly wrong. Reaching for the top shelf is what I need. I should be arranging my kitchen to make things more difficult. This is kitchen as metaphor, of course, for whatever the workshop of one's daily life happens to be. The same principles apply: in a perverse way, convenience is the enemy.

RUNNING TO RUN

Daily exercise dosage: thirty minutes of elevated heart rate, taken daily, a magic bullet against the ills of modern life. That's actually how running starts for most of us. If we progress beyond that formula, it is because we discover an appetite that turns running into something more: a challenge, a security blanket, a fulfillment unavailable in otherwise sedentary lives. Dr. Kenneth Cooper has said that if you're running more than fifteen miles a week, you're running for something other than cardiovascular health. Yes. Exactly.

What that other is hardly matters. The arthritic learn to "move to move"—to keep moving in order to maintain quality of movement. The luckier runners quickly find they run to run. Once that happens, they also begin to run in order to be able to run more.

This kind of circular rationale isn't about to satisfy science. One may not, in science, enjoy things for themselves. There has to be some measurable transaction, a receptor site, a means of transmission. No matter how good a time you're having, science is not amused. Working psychologists have discovered that running lowers anxiety, reduces anger and hostility, enhances self-esteem. What it does is no mystery; it's the why that drives science crazy.

For a while they thought it was a drug high: endorphins, the endogenous painkillers produced by hard effort. Nice theory, and a natural one in an increasingly drug-oriented society, but it never tested out. Depressives who are cheered up when they exercise aren't cheered up when they're just given endorphins. Without the accompanying work, our self-administered drug fix doesn't do the job.

Now they're looking at synaptic transmission. Depression is thought to be an imbalance at the neurotransmitter level: too much or too little of the various juices that carry messages across the synaptic gaps. Treatments that enhance synaptic transmission help alleviate depression. Shock treatment is one of those treatments. Running is another. Not all exercise does it: softball and tennis, for example, are much less effective in lifting depression.

I think that's because softball and tennis don't give enough repetitive work to the long muscles, and thus to the gamma system. Someday the search for the source of running's mood enhancers will get around to the gamma system—that neural loop that maintains muscle tone. Stimulation of the hypothalamus—the gland that governs mood—stimulates the gamma system, increasing muscle tone. That's how your mental attitude shows in your physical attitude. When you're depressed, you slump with what looks like fatigue but really isn't; when you're bright-eyed and bushy-tailed you show it in every move you make: in the muscles themselves, in the way they work. This isn't pseudoscientific "body language," it's right there in the wiring.

Although working the long muscles also fires the gamma system, for some reason it isn't supposed to stimulate the hypothalamus. That is, scientists have traced how the mental affects the physical, but can't seem to find their way back to where they started. Science is very big on one-way loops. The human body is not.

To us cheery runners, it hardly makes a difference where the kick comes from. The amusing part of the quandary, to me, is that depressives are considered the polar opposite of runners. I like what that says about us.

UNIFIED FIELD THEORY

Sometimes sports science seems to be trying to come up with a unified field theory of athletics, to reduce everything to oxygen consumed or calories burned or perhaps foot-pounds of energy exerted. It is perfectly conceivable, for instance, that the winner in the marathon might in fact turn out to be the person who can consume the most liters of oxygen per kilogram of body weight (as VO_2 max is usually expressed) for however long it takes to run the race.

There are runners who train and race that

way. They calculate what splits they'll have to run to post satisfactory times, what workouts they'll need to have under their belts to be able to run those splits, what maximum body weight they'll be able to carry and maintain the pace, what volume of liquids they'll need to replenish to keep their core temperature manageable. For all I know, they calculate how many steps they'll get per pair of shoe soles. When race day comes they are confident, knowing that they have cranked out the numbers in training. All they have to do in the race is fill in the rest of the numbers. If they don't win, it's because the numbers were wrong.

Some of them are very successful with this approach. Why do I keep thinking they're not having as much fun as the rest of us?

BALANCE

Fall running for me is vacation time: time to get off the road and into the woods. Then your running turns into a way of getting somewhere, of taking you to nice places so you can look at beautiful stuff. Forget about distance, measure your run by time alone: half the available minutes going out, half coming back. The workout will be just as good.

You'll have to revise your ideas about pace. Unsure footing may make it difficult to push very hard. Also, the woods provide a lot of distraction (which is what a vacation is supposed to do, right?). The thing that invariably seduces me is a rocky streambed: I can't resist the opportunity to explore one, wet or dry. I head up it at a dogtrot, mostly because I love the hypnotic demands of darting from stone to stone. It is not so much running as it is leaping from foot to foot: not a cardiovascular workout but a drill—in foot speed, concentration, reaction time. And balance, above all balance.

Dynamic, not static balance: the very thing that makes it fun is that you never quite do get a firm hold on your balance. You don't want to. A straight-line path is impossible; the next stone that is within reach and that offers decent footing is never quite in the direction you want to go. You switch back and forth like a hyperactive compass needle, vectoring your way. If you ever do catch up with your balance and get your weight stabilized, you stall on that rock, momentarily stuck. Getting started again wastes time and energy. So you're always predicting the direction of the step after next, never quite reaching equilibrium, banking your momentum off in a new direction. The faster you go, the steeper the banking; the better you predict, the less the effort, the greater the efficiency. Your body weight becomes something you catch and toss with each foot, and you dance—searching hard for a workable rhythm, inventing a new beat every third or fourth step —as you go. When you really get it going, it's not like running so much as it is working out with a light punching bag—using your feet instead of your fists.

Usually we run for our heart and lungs; running up a creek bed is running for our feet and ankles (and brain-spine system). This is the act of running turned upside down, somehow. That's what makes it such a nice change. It puts you thinking about balance in a new way. It may remind you to pay attention to the other kind of balance: mixing things up a bit to keep yourself fresh, to prevent the kind of grind that gets boring. Which, now that I think about it, was the reason I started running in the woods in the first place.

BIG VEINS

Roger, a friend and fellow runner, is on the phone when our conversation is interrupted by the buzz of the oven timer. My wife is working late, I don't feel like cooking, and he's caught me in the act of thawing some kind of Mexican-flavored glop for my solitary dinner. I find myself spinning out an elaborate rationale.

"It's okay," he says, "you probably have big veins."

Note the lack of scientific hair-splitting about things like cholesterol levels, plaque buildup, percentage of body fat. Roger knows his exercise physiology, but he doesn't bother even with such niceties as the difference between arteries and veins. He simply paints the quickest, clearest, most graphic picture he can. You've got these tubes in your chest, and as long as stuff can flow through them, you're okay. You've probably got enough room in there: sure, go ahead and pump a little more grease through. It'll probably go just fine.

I particularly enjoy this kind of economy of expression. It is shade-tree language, product of a mind in search of the most direct transmission of the thought: workingman's language, much valued among people who deal directly with the physical world. It is the language of locker rooms (which isn't necessarily blue). I think of it as essentially masculine, although some women speak it more clearly than men do. Nuts-and-bolts language.

Roger's background is southern, and includes army combat as well as athletics, although you hear none of those things in his speech. The only giveaway to that heritage is, occasionally, this entertaining directness of expression. Roger now lives in New England, interestingly enough, where this style of discourse is its own peculiar art form. As in that quintessential piece of New England advice about dealing with material matters: use it up, wear it out, make it do, or do without.

I'm sure Roger's running displays the same physical economy as his speech, although I've never seen him run. (He runs much too far and fast for me.) The same cast of mind that hones its discourse in the direction of efficiency is also going to hone athletic style, and in the same direction: in search of directness, conservation of energy, more effective application of force.

Wasted words are in fact wasted motions.

Roger and I may be fond of that style of communication out of nostalgia. We are both sedentary writers for much of the time, and perhaps may be forgiven an occasional wistful longing for the concreteness and accuracy of the world of physical forces. I miss it regularly. Pushing paper around (or, worse, blips of light on a screen) is not physically satisfying. That's a big part of why I exercise, I suspect—to vent the urge to expend a little gross-motor energy at something that will give an immediate and observable outcome. To move things a bit, even if those things are only my legs. But I've never asked Roger about his reasons.

Anyway, lunch-bucket language is a great vehicle for conveying succinct advice, and Roger's wisecrack deserves the legendary status it has achieved in our household. Now when I reach for the butter or a second helping, when I grab another beer or commit some other dietary sin, I hear it echo like a Greek chorus in the back of my head. Big veins? I'm considering having that engraved on a small brass plate for the refrigerator door.

"The correction of obesity in an affluent, sedentary society should not focus on decreased energy intake. Rather it should emphasize greater energy expenditure."

—*New England Journal of Medicine*

WAVES

Funny how fatigue can come in waves. You know the ones. You're rolling along just fine and then for no discernible reason your level of tiredness starts calling attention to itself. It feels like you've picked up the pace but you haven't; you're tempted to ease off a bit until the particular unpleasantness passes, but it isn't necessary. It only lasts for a little while. You can run through it. It is only a small blip in your physiological response. Your level of fitness hasn't changed, the pace is within your capacity, but you've got some system temporarily out of rhythm—your legs ahead of your lungs, too much tension carried somewhere, or too much pressure applied somewhere else. The disrhythm makes you feel suddenly tired until things get balanced out again.

PERCEIVED EFFORT

Pardon me if I keep making fun of the numerical approach to exercise. It's not intended as an attack on science, which has given us much wonderful new information to guide our running lives, but as a reminder that there are sometimes better indicators than numbers by which to judge our efforts. As a matter of fact, one better index has already been found. Perceived effort—the individual's own estimate of how hard he or she is working—is about as accurate an index to heart rate, and therefore to the threshold of the training effect, as anything the more numbers-oriented types have ever come up with.

In other words, if it feels like you're working moderately hard, you probably are. There's a school of scientific thought that holds that this is about as much information as we actually need.

ON BECOMING GREEN

Most runners I know have a sincere concern for preserving the environment. It occurs to me that their environmental awareness might be a natural outgrowth of their interest in fitness.

We run in order to return ourselves to fitness; the aim of the environmental movement is to perform the same kind of recuperative work on the earth itself: to achieve, or restore, its physical fitness.

And it seems entirely logical that the point where the fitness and the environmental movements would come together should be in the outdoors. After all, that's where we run.

EXAMINING THE DATA

ASSUME ALL ATHLETES HAVE HEART DISEASE, reads the headline. The advice comes from a cardiologist, of course, at a conference on sports medicine. "Physicians should assume that all adults seeking medical examinations to participate in strenuous sports probably have coronary artery disease." The incidence of heart problems in this country is high enough, he claims, to warrant so bleak an approach. Isn't it funny how when you're a hammer everything looks like a nail?

This particular cardiologist says that taking a good medical history and examining for specific problems—blood pressure abnormalities, heart murmur, arrhythmias—is sufficient. Other, even more pessimistic medical advisers, would have you take a stress test. There are also scientists who say stress tests won't reveal the real problems anyway; that requires an angiogram—which can, in rare cases, be fatal. What is a runner to make of this expert advice?

As a journalist who has studied these matters, it's my job to resolve these contradictions. Examine the data, raise the proper questions. Does it make sense, for instance, to modify our behavior on the basis of information collected from the population of Framingham, Massachusetts, or from Harvard alumni, as the two largest studies have done? If not these people, whom should we study? Runners? What's a "runner"? Five miles a week, thirty, a hundred? I've had two stress tests, years apart; both gave me a clean bill of health and, vastly relieved, I increased my training. Was this relief warranted? My wife, who has a heart murmur, also had a stress test, and was advised to keep right on running but not to compete. But then she also found a dietitian who told her butter was okay. Something's gone wrong here, but I can't get my mind around it. I'm fogged out anyway—head spinning, unable to think. I'll go for a run.

It's a brisk, cool day, and, buoyed along, almost bouncing down the road, my mood immediately begins to improve. I needed this, I think, and begin to change, in my head, from plodding runner to fleeing animal. The breeze, too chilly when I started, is welcome when I turn back toward home. Gradually I slow, and then walk the last four hundred yards. As I do, some different kind of warmth starts humming through my muscles, my very veins. Call it well-being, for want of a better word.

The subjective pleasure of that hum by itself probably won't make me live longer. Science says it's what one does to make the hum happen that accomplishes that: the objective part, miles run, calories burned. Okay, I accept this. I even need the objective part, to let me know what I've done, what I need to do. Besides, it helps to remind me, when my head is too full of other things, of the subjective pleasures that lie just outside my door.

I spend too many hours with my head whirling and my body still, forgetting how that situation can be reversed anytime I want. Sorry, but I can't sort out the conflicting advice. Medical science can't seem to make up its mind what it wants from—or for—us runners. Until it does, I'm happy using running for purposes other than longevity. I use it to set my body whirling, and thereby still my head.

FASHION STATEMENT

One of the things that pleases me most about running is that when you're doing it, things are what they are and nothing more. Clothes are to protect your skin and keep you warm enough, period. I love the thoughtful design and high quality of the new running gear, but the colors make me nuts. Magenta and neon green don't seem playful to me, they seem to be saying, hey, look at me. As Thoreau put it, beware all enterprises that require new clothes. If I want my clothes to make a statement, I'll wear a piece of writing. The new running gear is great; now how about making it in colors for nonstarlets?

PUTTING IT BACK

Runners breathe a lot. Running makes us breathe more. Run too fast and we quickly become a lot more interested in breathing than in continuing to run: running out of breath is the one thing, short of orthopedic injury, that will most quickly drag us to a halt. How much air we can suck into our lungs is in fact the single most important factor in determining pace.

Not surprisingly, science has paid a lot of attention to the breath. At least eight different lung-volume measurements can be taken, the most important of which is vital capacity. What a great term! It is defined as the maximal volume that can be forcefully expired after maximal inspiration; if any respiratory measurement is taken during a physical exam, vital capacity will usually be the one. It is an important index of aging (thus the comic actor, playing an old duffer who can't blow out all those candles on his birthday cake). Runners of course have greater vital capacity, and generally higher other respiratory measurements, than nonrunners.

Like running, breathing is a muscular task, more complicated than it feels. The lungs have no muscles of their own. In normal use, we expand the lungs by contracting the diaphragm (the sheet of muscle that separates chest from abdominal cavity), and the exterior layer of intercostal muscles, which lift and rotate the ribs. Contracting these various muscles increases the volume of the chest cavity, sucking air into the lungs. The lungs and chest cavity are elastic, and expanding them stores energy; when we relax, that elasticity powers the exhale. For the exhale, no effort required.

That's for resting respiration. To get more air we have to spend more energy; when we're really pumping, we contract muscles of the upper chest, throat, back, and even the neck in order to further expand the chest volume. Under extreme demands we have to burn energy to pump the air out again, contracting the inner layer of intercostal muscles (pulling the ribs together) and tightening the abdomen to force the diaphragm upward. During heavy exercise, these respiratory muscles may consume an amazing eight to ten percent of the total amount of oxygen we're using.

We only borrow air, of course—can't take it in without eventually giving it back—but we change it while we're using it, consuming oxygen and producing carbon dioxide. As runners we're even a bit greedy, getting out there every day and burning up as much oxygen as we can cram into our lungs. Not as much as an automobile driver, perhaps—or a cigarette smoker—but we're part of the problem. Maybe we should grow things to replace the oxygen we're consuming: use the atmosphere, but give back some of it, too.

The mystics have always known the breath's centering effect; runners may get the same benefit but get it faster, harder. Breathing, after all, is life's single most sustaining activity—and it is breath itself that is so enhanced by running. Running makes you breathe, gets you to breathe, gives you a chance to breathe more. That's a benefit the fitness folks forget to tell you about.

TAKE THAT, PAIN

Coaches always tell you to listen to your body. Unfortunately, in some ways training decreases rather than enhances your ability to do that. This may reduce your level of hypochondria, but it can cause you to miss some fairly important signals.

In fact a lot of the masters (aka overage) athletes use physical effort as a way of numbing themselves out. They're not so much holding off age as trying to dull its discomforts. As aging's messages get more urgent, they are saying to their physiology, "You call that pain? I'll show you pain." It's a process of toughening up almost in the dendritic sense: growing bark. It's also where overuse injuries come from.

FOR FUN

Age tries to stiffen us from the center outward: spine, thoracic chamber, pelvic girdle, all trying to turn to concrete. These symptoms are not the result of age itself but of too many sedentary hours. Aging is a disease of hypokinesis—literally, not enough movement. One antidote, then, is hyperkinesis, or exercise. Running or any other form of active motion that suits your fancy will do just fine. In addition to the benefits that accrue to the waistline, coronary arteries, and mental health, there's also resistance to aging. For some of us that's the most important reason of all for running.

What we have here is another cerebral argument for the physical life. Unfortunately, argument never talked anyone into physicality, for the same reason that nagging at yourself to stand up straight doesn't cure slumped shoulders. The only way you're going to change your posture is by sensation: you have to fall in love with what it feels like to stand up straight. Your head won't remind you to stand up straight; your back and shoulders have to do it. Your physical awareness has to do it. The message must come from nerve endings farther from the brain—and it has to come as pleasure, not aggravation.

As with slumped shoulders, so with the sedentary life. The toughest possible way to make an exercise program work is by argument: on a doctor's advice, to avoid heart problems, to make yourself sexier, to fit your clothes better. The easiest way is to surrender to the body's impulse to move more: to sate an appetite, rather than to deny one. Follow the pleasure principle. The funny thing is, you start being physical just for fun and—as all runners eventually come to know—then it gets interesting. That's where the cerebral part comes in.

PROBLEM-SOLVING

Keeping exercise fresh is the habitual runner's daily task. One intriguing way of doing that is to look at every run as a set of physiological problems to solve: where, this time, will you put the load, the will, the effort? When do you attack, when do you coast? How do you choose to manage the heat or the cold, the footing, the traffic? How do you divide the task between the cardiovascular and musculoskeletal systems?

Some of these problems are solved with the head (the intelligence) and some with the body (brute force); all of them are finally solved by proprioception, I think. Or by all the senses—by the entire sensory universe—proprioception being the one sense that makes all the others available.

Proprioception is that miraculous self-sensing mechanism of the human organism that tells us whether we are in motion or at rest, that even tells us where we are and what we're doing. It measures movement, direction, acceleration, and deceleration. It is the sense that gives us a self to take for runs. It is the sense, I think, that makes us whole.

POOPED

You know the feeling: you've done something gloriously exhausting, spent a really demanding day; you lie down to sleep and for the first five minutes you hurt all over. You wonder if you haven't actually done something harmful to yourself.

Then that generalized pain changes over to the delicious glow of recovery, and you plunge down into sleep, knowing you've accomplished as much as you can physically with your conscious self, and now must turn things over to the healing properties of rest. You give up your consciousness like throwing your hat in the air. I love that feeling. It is available only to people who explore the shores of exhaustion regularly, who are in good enough health to recover quickly. Regular running makes you one of those people.

DISCERNMENT

When I was training hard I would consistently be over the edge, tumbling down the well into overtraining, before my body would admit I was even getting tired. My shoulders somehow acquired a full-blown case of tendinitis without my ever noticing it—until too late, of course. When my body tried to speak, I had somehow turned stone deaf.

Not unusual: I once attended a national festival of masters athletes, where two or three thousand middle-aged folks gathered to compete in a dozen different sports. The two most striking things about them were how alert and alive they looked—how bright-eyed—and how many of them were limping. Systemically, these people were the picture of health; orthopedically, they were a disaster. Being healthy but injured seemed to be the natural state. We are not inclined, I think, to be too easy on ourselves.

Most of us actively train to overcome either the effects of a sedentary lifestyle or the effects of aging. To do so requires that you defy certain of those effects. Training necessarily teaches you to ignore, rather than heed, a good portion of the signals your body sends you. Remember how hard it was, when you were getting started as a runner, to push past those first alarms.

We're supposed to learn to discern which signals mean something and which don't, but few of us get very good at this discernment. So we choose to ignore everything.

In masters athletics what most people master first is the art of ignoring the obvious: how old they are. (We're not going to let that stop us.) We become masters at carrying on, at persevering, at getting in our mileage and getting through our races, come hell or high water. To do so, we've had to build up a fairly heavy pro-tective coating on our pain sensors. It's not easy to catch your body's subtle signals when you are essentially a callus from head to foot.

I never did learn the art of training hard and listening to my body at the same time. I'm not even sure "listening" is the right term—but I do know you can't do it very well if you have cal-luses over your ears. I never expected to cam-paign for undertraining, but if you're reading this, you may need to be encouraged to do less, rather than more. Listen or not (as it pleases you), to me or to your body, but whatever you do, don't lose all discernment of overtraining. That can hurt more in the long run.

THE OFFICIAL WORD

"Strength training of a moderate intensity, sufficient to develop and maintain fat-free weight, should be an integral part of an adult fitness program."

—American College of Sports Medicine

GOOFING OFF

December running is a test of character. To carry a disciplined running schedule through all its distractions is quite a severe test. Here's a somewhat heretical suggestion: save all of that self-discipline for the other eleven months. December ought to be goof-off time, time to ease up on yourself. Not without reason is the end of the year the time of the fun runs, inspired sillinesses, and midnight madnesses. You might as well join in: celebration is for runners, too.

WORKING AT PLAY,
PLAYING AT WORK

Play is work done for pleasure. Most of us work at play a lot harder than we work at work. To distinguish work from more vexatious labor, all we've been able to come up with is the unfortunate word *exercise.* How badly that term fails to capture the excitement and reward that hard use of the human body can bring.

SUGARPLUMS

Nutritionists have been telling us for years to fuel our running with complex carbohydrates rather than simple ones. Complex carbohydrates are pasta, bread, potatoes, and other starches; simple ones are, well, sugarish. You know: candy, cookies, ice cream. Cake and pie. Gooey stuff.

Now comes word (hooray!) that for carbohydrate-loading, anyway—as in preparation for a race—simple carbohydrates are better. Energy from simple carbohydrates is more quickly available to the working body. Why does this news make me think of a streetful of kids, dancing around the ice cream cart? Or bees plundering blossoms in springtime, or other examples of the milling, buzzing energy that living creatures always bring to bear when sweetness is made available?

I was a latchkey kid during World War II, and would come home from school, let myself in, and go straight to the kitchen, looking for something sweet. It never occurred to me to eat pure sugar, which was rationed (and a little decadent, somehow, in the bargain), but I can still remember the time, in about the third grade, when I stumbled onto a box of brown sugar. I dug out a hardened lump half the size of a golf ball and popped it into my mouth; it crunched deliciously, then melted. I can still taste it: one of the most satisfactory pieces of candy I ever had. It's a peculiar tribute to the power of sweetness, I think, that I remember with perfect clarity that particular chunk of sugar, that moment of biting down into it, after more than fifty years.

There is no shortage of argument against sugar. Some believe refined sugar to be a communist conspiracy. The stuff has certainly figured as a suspicious element of our foreign policy for decades. One has only to read the labels to discover that our supermarkets are stocked, aisle after aisle, with sugar-based products. Some would have us believe that sugar is an addictive drug, implicated in everything from tooth decay to hyperactivity in children.

There are even arguments over which kind of sugar we should eat. Nutritional faddists have tried to make the case for complex sugars for years—usually for honey over refined sugar, but sometimes for things like fructose (fruit sugar), for example, over sucrose. (Exercise physiologist Dave Costill points out that sugar is sugar, and the shape of the molecule it comes in doesn't make a particle of difference to the cells that end up putting it to use.) Certainly sugar is empty calories, and you do need other nutrition, and if you are getting sufficient nutrition from other sources the sugar will sure enough go directly onto your love handles. And all that, and all that.

But I keep thinking of the bees. I think we wouldn't have such expressions in the language as "sweetening the offer" if there weren't some deep, atavistic, natural lust for the stuff. Frankly, I've never been able to convince myself that sugar is all that terrible as a source of energy. But I may be prejudiced.

Naturally, then, I'm delighted that in this season when sugarplums are supposed to dance in our heads, along comes science and says we can also go ahead and put them in our mouths.

THE ANNALS OF SPAGHETTI, PART II

"Everything you see I owe to spaghetti."
—Sophia Loren

OBJECTIVE VS. SUBJECTIVE EATING

Let's apply the objective/subjective dichotomy to eating, the runner's second most favorite activity. (Okay, third most favorite.) Objective eating, let's say, has to do with the stuff you cram into yourself: what you need to maintain your health and weight, and to perform your best. It's where attention seems to be focused these days.

A lot of attention is being paid, too. All we really know about nutrition can be put into about five sentences, but there's at least one feature article on the subject in every issue of nearly every periodical published these days. Most of them are endless variations on that old theme of what you really ought to eat and how you ought to eat it. It's my contrarian nature, I suppose, but such talk makes me want to emit a sharp, snappy bark: get your nose out of my food bowl, diet police.

Feature articles about diet and nutrition usually manage to imply that if you'll just take their advice, miraculous results will follow. This is not new; we've been searching for dietary miracles since we added roots to the shopping

list to go along with those berries we'd been for-
aging for. We've never given up hope. We're
still searching for the elusive mix that will not
only taste great and be less filling but also fuel
us to new heights of physical and mental performance —not to mention clear up our skin.

Unfortunately for the prospect of miracles,
objective science has broken down all this food
business into units of heat and a few simple
chemicals—which is what the body does, too, of
course, in order to use it. At the level of heat and
chemistry, there are firm laws against miracles.
(Come to think of it, turning pasta into a 2:10
marathon ought to be miracle enough for anyone.) Eat a balanced diet—properly balanced in
terms of fuel intake versus energy expenditure,
in fat versus carbohydrates versus proteins, in
liquids, vitamins, and minerals—and you've
done all you can do to improve yourself by way
of your gullet. It's not all that complicated.

Until we get to subjective eating, which is
the part about how stuff tastes. That's when the
nutritional grenades start going off in our knap-
sacks. Trying to lower our intake of fats, we discover that's where all the flavor lies. Raise your
hand if you remember those glorious years
when red meat was "healthy protein." Now it

turns out that the protein part is as tasteless as cardboard, hard to chew, harder to swallow—and, in injudicious amounts, not good for you anyway. Then there are the hypertension alarmists, whose warnings alone are scary enough to raise your blood pressure: they're even trying to get us to cut out salt. You remember salt, don't you—that stuff that, losing its savor, makes life not worth living?

Subjective, or flavor-oriented, eating makes life tastier but shorter, according to the diet police. Possibly. Objective eating, on the other hand, may just make life seem longer. Subjective cooks transcend science in pursuit of art; objective cooks are stuck back there with the units of heat and chemical compounds. Lacking a full palate to get our attention, they're always tempted to venture beyond science. That's when nutrition turns into the New Astrology.

I don't know about you, but my sign is sucrose. Maybe it's these visions I've been having—the ones with the sugarplums.

The ultimate lesson in all this for runners is: eat hearty. Just make sure you run hearty, too.

INVULNERABILITY

Running can make you feel invulnerable, and that's dangerous if it leads to neglect of other decent health habits. But invulnerable is also a terrific way to feel. I think we runners have decided not to give that up.

YOUR CHOICE

Circumstances can keep you from running where and when you want, but nothing except lack of training can take away your right to run exactly as hard as you want to. The more you run, the more of this freedom you acquire. That's the beauty part.

CHOOSING YOUR PACE

When we talk about pace we're usually thinking of six-minute miles or eight-minute miles or some other way of measuring our speed down the road. For the lifetime runner, though, that kind of thinking about pace may be all wrong. The pace that counts is a longer one, the measuring unit of which is the year. You keep racking those up, as a runner, and you're getting about as much good as you possibly can from the sport.

To do so means to pick your pace from the earth in its journey around the sun. It is the longer of the two paces that are laid out for us by the solar system itself. The shorter of these is the day: a sprint, ripping by, at least from the astronomical point of view, like the numerals that flash the hundredths of a second on a digital stopwatch.

The other pace is the seasonal one, the year: the ponderous swaying back and forth of the earth as it spins, shining the direct light of the sun first on the Northern Hemisphere, then on the Southern one, and back again. Run to that rhythm. You'll run better for it.